Poems of the Decade
An anthology of the Forward books of poetry

This anthology was designed and produced by Bookmark (formerly Forward Worldwide), sponsor of the Forward Prizes. Bookmark is a global content and communications company based in London, Toronto, Montreal, Santiago, Lima, New York, LA, Shanghai and Singapore. Bookmark uses consumer insights to develop compelling content for brands that engages consumers and drives sales. Clients include Patek Philippe, Air Canada, LATAM, Bombardier, Fairmont Hotels & Resorts, Explora, Standard Life, Tesco, American Express Travel, Mercedes-Benz, Christie's, Lindt, the Academy of St Martin in the Fields and StreetSmart. bookmarkcontent.com @bookmarkcontent

Poems of the Decade
An anthology of the
Forward books of poetry

BOOKM/ARK

LONDON

First published in Great Britain by
Forward Worldwide Ltd, now Bookmark,
in association with
Faber and Faber · Bloomsbury House · 74–77 Great Russell Street
London WC1B 3DA

ISBN 978 0 571 32540 5 (paperback)

Printed and bound by CPI Group (UK) · Croydon CR0 4YY

A CIP catalogue reference for this book
is available at the British Library.

To Felicity Ann Sieghart with love and thanks

Contents

Preface

TREAT THIS ANTHOLOGY WITH CAUTION. It looks harmless, but contains multitudes: works that speak of violence, danger and fear alongside love and longing, in forms broken and reshaped by the need to communicate what it is to be alive now, here.

Beyond this book lie ten Forward anthologies of poetry, one for each year of the millennium's first decade. And beyond them? Many hundreds of slim volumes and thousands of single poems submitted to the Forward Prizes for Poetry in that time.

The Prizes were first awarded in 1992 by a young entrepreneur, William Sieghart, who wanted to find a way of discovering and sharing whatever good poetry was being written at the time. It is easy for a curious mind to learn of the most exciting movies, music, novels and artworks created in recent years, he reasoned. Why should poetry be any different?

Sieghart's idea was simple: in the spring, he invited publishers to send their 'best' recent poetry books to a five-strong panel of judges, then invited the judges to choose the ones that lodged most vividly in their minds over the summer. And in the autumn, three prizes were awarded: Best Collection, Best First Collection and Best Single Poem. A selection of the shortlisted and highly commended poems were then collected in the first *Forward Book of Poetry*. This happened again. And again. New judges. New winners. New readers. After a decade, during which he founded National Poetry Day, Sieghart plucked his favourite poems for a Forward book of books. Now that's happened again, too. The judging doesn't stop and start: it continues. We hope you join in the work of sifting, choosing, celebrating as readers: for ideas on how to do this, go to the Forward Arts Foundation website and social media feeds.

There are poems here by authors who have long been famous: Seamus Heaney, Carol Ann Duffy, Simon Armitage. Others deserve to be far better known. But none is in by chance: each work was chosen because a phrase, a sound, an image or pattern alerted a judge to something happening – something important and interesting, quite possibly in the gap between one line and the next. Forward Prizes judges are themselves poets, musicians, actors, journalists, writers and artists: none reads a poem in quite the same way as another. They argue as they cast their nets, and sometimes for many years afterwards.

If you wonder which of these poems are prize-winners, turn to the back of the book. They may not be the poems, or indeed poets, you expect. A writer you rate highly may not figure in the roll of honour, and vice versa. And if this surprises and annoys you, then welcome to the big conversation about poetry and taste. For whatever the claims made at the moment of judgment, few poetry juries would be rash enough, years later, to insist that their time-pressured verdicts are definitive or beyond dispute. How could they be? The formation of a canon takes years and involves the thoughts of many: taste may possibly be shaped by five eminent creative and critical minds in a book-lined room, but it cannot be controlled. The days when a poem could be anointed from on high as 'great' – and accepted serenely without argument – are over, if they ever existed.

Grayson Perry allowed the use of an image of his pot *Language of Cars* on the cover: his kindness will seem all the more remarkable to anyone who reads Tim Turnbull's Keatsian ode on a Grayson urn on page 172.

We thank Forward Worldwide, loyal and generous supporters of the Forward Prizes since the start, particularly Casey Jones, Will Scott and Christopher Stocks who produce the Forward anthologies. Ben Sinyor's extraordinary care and attention to detail made this revised edition possible. Arts Council England, the Esmée Fairbairn Foundation, the John Ellerman Foundation and the Rothschild Foundation all fund us to celebrate excellence in poetry and widen its audience through the Forward Prizes and National Poetry Day. Thank you to each.

And finally, thanks to our founder chairman William Sieghart, whose curiosity and passion continue to drive the Forward Arts Foundation.

January 2015   Susannah Herbert
                                          Executive Director, Forward Arts Foundation

www.forwardartsfoundation.org
@forwardprizes
facebook.com/forwardprizes

Poems of the Decade
An anthology of the
Forward books of poetry

Patience Agbabi

Eat Me

When I hit thirty, he brought me a cake,
three layers of icing, home-made,
a candle for each stone in weight.

The icing was white but the letters were pink,
they said, EAT ME. And I ate, did
what I was told. Didn't even taste it.

Then he asked me to get up and walk
round the bed so he could watch my broad
belly wobble, hips judder like a juggernaut.

The bigger the better, he'd say, *I like*
big girls, soft girls, girls I can burrow inside
with multiple chins, masses of cellulite.

I was his Jacuzzi. But he was my cook,
my only pleasure the rush of fast food,
his pleasure, to watch me swell like forbidden fruit.

His breadfruit. His desert island after shipwreck.
Or a beached whale on a king-size bed
craving a wave. I was a tidal wave of flesh

too fat to leave, too fat to buy a pint of full-fat milk,
too fat to use fat as an emotional shield,
too fat to be called chubby, cuddly, big-built.

The day I hit thirty-nine, I allowed him to stroke
my globe of a cheek. His flesh, my flesh flowed.
He said, *Open wide*, poured olive oil down my throat.

Soon you'll be forty... he whispered, and how
could I not roll over on top. I rolled and he drowned
in my flesh. I drowned his dying sentence out.

I left him there for six hours that felt like a week.
His mouth slightly open, his eyes bulging with greed.
There was nothing else left in the house to eat.

Ann Alexander

Dead Cat Poem

She who flowed like mercury, or mist
over silent fields,
who had seen off foxes,
terrorized hedgerows, endangered
several species of rodent,
was now sitting on death's lap
and feeling his cold fingers.

We stood and looked for signs of her
in the grey bundle we had petted and stroked
lugged and loved through the years.
But she was looking elsewhere,
untidy for the first time,
dusty and in disarray.

Strange that when we buried her
beneath a flowering bush, in the sunny place
where she loved to sit,
we could not touch her.
Scooped her up with a spade.

Simon Armitage

CHAINSAW VERSUS THE PAMPAS GRASS

It seemed an unlikely match. All winter unplugged,
grinding its teeth in a plastic sleeve, the chainsaw swung
nose-down from a hook in the darkroom
under the hatch in the floor. When offered the can
it knocked back a quarter-pint of engine oil
and juices ran from its joints and threads,
oozed across the guide-bar and the maker's name,
into the dry links.

From the summerhouse, still holding one last gulp
of last year's heat behind its double doors, and hung
with the weightless wreckage of wasps and flies,
moth-balled in spider's wool…
from there, I trailed the day-glo orange power-line
the length of the lawn and the garden path,
fed it out like powder from a keg, then walked
back to the socket and flicked the switch, then walked again
and coupled the saw to the flex – clipped them together.
Then dropped the safety catch and gunned the trigger.

No gearing up or getting to speed, just an instant rage,
the rush of metal lashing out at air, connected to the main.
The chainsaw with its perfect disregard, its mood
to tangle with cloth, or jewellery, or hair.
The chainsaw with its bloody desire, its sweet tooth
for the flesh of the face and the bones underneath,
its grand plan to kick back against nail or knot
and rear up into the brain.
I let it flare, lifted it into the sun
and felt the hundred beats per second drumming in its heart,
and felt the drive-wheel gargle in its throat.

The pampas grass with its ludicrous feathers
and plumes. The pampas grass, taking the warmth and light
from cuttings and bulbs, sunning itself,
stealing the show with its footstools, cushions and tufts
and its twelve-foot spears.

This was the sledgehammer taken to crack the nut.
Probably all that was needed here was a good pull or shove
or a pitchfork to lever it out at its base.
Overkill. I touched the blur of the blade
against the nearmost tip of a reed – it didn't exist.
I dabbed at a stalk that swooned, docked a couple of heads,
dismissed the top third of its canes with a sideways sweep
at shoulder height – this was a game.
I lifted the fringe of undergrowth, carved at the trunk –
plant-juice spat from the pipes and tubes
and dust flew out as I ripped into pockets of dark, secret
     warmth.

To clear a space to work
I raked whatever was severed or felled or torn
towards the dead zone under the outhouse wall, to be fired.
Then cut and raked, cut and raked, till what was left
was a flat stump the size of a manhole cover or barrel lid
that wouldn't be dug with a spade or prized from the earth.
Wanting to finish things off I took up the saw
and drove it vertically downwards into the upper roots,
but the blade became choked with soil or fouled with weeds,
or what was sliced or split somehow closed and mended
     behind,
like cutting at water or air with a knife.
I poured barbecue fluid into the patch
and threw in a match – it flamed for a minute, smoked
for a minute more, and went out. I left it at that.

In the weeks that came new shoots like asparagus tips
sprang up from its nest and by June
it was riding high in its saddle, wearing a new crown.
Corn in Egypt. I looked on
from the upstairs window like the midday moon.

Back below stairs on its hook, the chainsaw seethed.
I left it a year, to work back through its man-made dreams,
to try to forget.
The seamless urge to persist was as far as it got.

Tiffany Atkinson

ZUPPA DI CECI

In chipped English she told me

that to get mine like hers   Well

      I'm just too flash-in-the-pan

These things take time   Chick-peas alone

      must be soaked overnight   then simmered for hours

while you stand at the stove with a slow spoon

      skimming off scum   only then a hope in hell

you'll get the rest of the ingredients to sit

      on the right staves   Though

what this has to do with you

      slipping out in the crease of night like

a dropped stitch   I can't think   just

      the kitchen window's black slab

where I stand sucking cream from the lip

      of an old spoon   a platter of reheated stars

and last night's moon served cold

Ros Barber

MATERIAL

My mother was the hanky queen
when hanky meant a thing of cloth,
not paper tissues bought in packs
from late-night garages and shops,
but things for waving out of trains
and mopping the corners of your grief:
when hankies were material
she'd have one, always, up her sleeve.

Tucked in the wrist of every cardi,
a mum's embarrassment of lace
embroidered with a V for Viv,
spittled and scrubbed against my face.
And sometimes more than one fell out
as if she had a farm up there
where dried-up hankies fell in love
and mated, raising little squares.

She bought her own; I never did.
Hankies were presents from distant aunts
in boxed sets, with transparent covers
and script initials spelling *ponce*,
the naffest Christmas gift you'd get –
my brothers too, more often than not,
got male ones: serious, and grey,
and larger, like they had more snot.

It was hankies that closed department stores,
with headscarves, girdles, knitting wool
and trouser presses; homely props
you'd never find today in malls.
Hankies, which demanded irons,
and boiling to be purified

shuttered the doors of family stores
when those who used to buy them died.

And somehow, with the hanky's loss,
greengrocer George with his dodgy foot
delivering veg from a Comma van
is history, and the friendly butcher
who'd slip an extra sausage in,
the fishmonger whose marble slab
of haddock smoked the colour of yolks
and parcelled rows of local crab

lay opposite the dancing school
where Mrs White, with painted talons,
taught us *When You're Smiling* from
a stumbling, out of tune piano:
step-together, step-together, step-together,
point! The Annual Talent Show
when every mother, fencing tears,
would whip a hanky from their sleeve
and smudge the rouge from little dears.

Nostalgia only makes me old.
The innocence I want my brood
to cling on to like ten-bob notes
was killed in TV's lassitude.
And it was me that turned it on
to buy some time to write this poem
and eat bought biscuits I would bake
if I'd commit to being home.

There's never a hanky up my sleeve.
I raised neglected-looking kids,
the kind whose noses strangers clean.
What awkwardness in me forbids
me to keep tissues in my bag
when handy packs are 50p?

I miss material handkerchiefs,
their soft and hidden history.

But it isn't mine. I'll let it go.
My mother too, eventually,
who died not leaving handkerchiefs
but tissues and uncertainty:
and she would say, should I complain
of the scratchy and disposable,
that *this is your material
to do with, daughter, what you will.*

Edward Barker

CRYSTAL NIGHT

In my father's house
paper was always at a premium.
I arrived one night,
it must have been raining for weeks
and even the floors were soggy –
like those of a used ark.
It had a way of provoking images, references,
this house, uncontrollably.

He was sitting by the fire.
I sat down on the broken armchair
next to him – the light of the flames
flickering in his stone-age cheeks.
He tossed another book into the fire.

I smiled, and glanced at the woodpile –
what was there was sodden, unburnable.
No one had been out to gather wood.

He was burning selectively, a kind of literary
criticism. Trying not to appear fascinated
I checked the burnt and burning spines,
I remember there was a Heyer and wondered
if he had gone off her. A couple of phone
books. Fortunately no history.

He was enjoying himself. I saw a Gideon
on the pile next to him. I said nothing,
not wishing to give him grounds to provoke.
So far no poems in the fire either.

We sat chatting. I wondered whether he
remembered. Suddenly I remembered

he must have been 21 when it happened.
Not likely he would forget.

I also realized I had seen
the same newsreel that he must have,
the one with the ruddy faces
cheerfully throwing armfuls of books
onto the bonfire, the campsite songs.

And I knew his was a coded message,
a sort of Mafia communication.
As we chatted of this and that
I tried to work out what he was saying:

could have been – we're living through
it all over again – but that was too crude.
Or – you've abandoned me and this
is how I survive now – but he was too
proud and different for that. Maybe he
was showing me what it was like.
But he was just enjoying himself.
The books burned on.

It seemed as if the words, released
by the flames, flew up chaotically
into the chimney. It was clear
letters and phrases, scorched,
were getting stuck in the blackened
brickwork and creating entirely new
patterns, even poems.

From a distance I imagined
you could see the house, its chimney
spewing words in clouds over the
fields, into the stream, the trees.
A truly literary house.

Judi Benson

Burying the Ancestors

I

I'm tired of being crooned to the tune
of old Aunt Liza's dead goose,
lullabyed in those cotton fields back home,
roused to Dixie, swamped in the Sewanee River,
hearing Mammy say *hush chile*,
you know your Mamma was born to die.
The one they called Morning, born into the light,
taking her mamma's life. *Hush chile. Hush Mammy.*

I want the repeat names to stop repeating,
all those Henry fathers, greats and grands,
uncles, brothers, cousins intertwined, intermarried.
Juniors, Seniors, and all those Roman numerals, just delete.

Set fire to the tissue-thin letters of fine penmanship
and not much to say, *weather's fine,*
coming home in the covered wagon.
Clip the stamps, give them to the collector,
then burn baby burn.

Burn all their blusterings, their justifications
for blistering others' skin in the relentless summer heat,
while they wrapped themselves around shady porches.

I know to honour this blood flowing through me
is to say nothing. Don't mention the wills
begetting slaves and all their increase, forever, amen.
Sadie, Cicely, Moses, Caesar, and the one they called Patience.
Chains around their necks, chains around their ankles,
chains around their hopeless hearts,
all for the increase of those who refused to work the land,
whose hands were forbidden to touch dirt.

But my tongue wants to be released from its stays.
All those big hats bouncing with flowers, tossed in the wind,
pale faces unveiled, finding a trace of the darker hue hinted at.

II

Let Eugenia in her ball gown go waltzing
back out the door. Stop fanning her lashes at the Judge,
begging him to pass the Secession Act on her birthday.
Pretty please Judge, I'll be 19. And so he did,
slicing Georgia off from the Union.

And then what, and what if only Johnny
had come marching home again.
Eugenia, dead of night, bundling her babies
into the flat wagon, crossing the rising river,
just before the bridge gave out,
whipping the horses and cursing those damn Yankees
she'd never forgive, nor all her increase.

Eugenia always seen in mourning-black,
burying her father, her babies, her husband.
Rocking on her porch, silver-haired,
a black ribbon round her neck, glint in her eye,
sure the South would rise again.

III

Soft people, hard people, lines crissing and crossing
the economic divide, rattling at the edges of china cups,
hands cracked from hard work, soft hands slipping into gloves.
Ladies and Gents, rebels and ruffians.

These strangers: Benjamin, Lydia, Josh and Jasmine,
flattened in the black and white photograph,
sitting stiffly, even when casual,
suspicious of the man under black cloth
the little box with the sudden *Pop!*
Smile? Say cheese? What's that.

Meat? No one's had any in months,
cracked corn, bucked wheat,
and always hoe cake, though once
it was told, syrup.

Once the land was fertile.
Then grew to be like its people, over-worked, exhausted,
tobacco, cotton, corn, thirsty for rain.
The great greats and not-so-greats
with their sharp pulled-back hair,
tight knots, tributaries of trouble
running across their faces,
bending their mouths down,
bones edging through the little skin.
Even the old-eyed children
clench an angry desperation in their faces.

Left-overs, that was all some could afford to rent.
All they had, they'd inherited, the feather bed,
one scrawny mule, three slaves and all their increase.
Just another mouth to feed.

IV

Planters, plantation owners, preachers, politicians,
doctors, lawyers, artists, teachers, n'er do wells, drunks,
do-gooders, glamour girls posing for Coca Cola ads:
Camille, Vally, Lamar,
naughty girls seen smoking in public, racey women,
swell men, bootleg whisky, speakeasys, suicides,
insanity, vanity and humility. Anecdotes and ancient history,
all it boils down to. Stories told, changed in the telling.

Henry was driving through the back roads in his Model T,
so fast he killed a bunch of chickens on the dusty Georgia clay.
'Hey Mister, you gotta pay,' shouts the irate farmer.
'How much?' 'Make it fifteen bucks.'
'Here's 30 cause I'm comin back just as fast.'

Little Henry, Big Henry, dead Henry.

Some lost to sea, some to land. War heroes,
influenza victims, gamblers, ladies' men,
loose women, tight-laced Baptists, Huguenots,
shouting Methodists,
Klan members and Abolitionists,
Suffragettes and Southern Belles,
side by side now, bones mouldering together,
mixing up the arguments, leaving all that love hanging.

v

They were just people, sugah, father said,
they worked hard and were honest. Religious folk,
never played cards on Sunday, never mixed with coloreds.
Amen. Praise the Lord and pass the ammunition,
pass the succotash, pass the buck, cross yourself,
swear to tell the truth, pray the Lord your soul to take
and all that hate: Absalom, Walter, Kitty, Caroline,
Dolly with the hole in her stocking, dance with her,
dance with all her dead. Jason with the hole in his head, fix it.
The named and never named, the never talked about one
who ran away with the chauffeur, the older one who stayed,
the one forever missing in action,
the ones whose minds flew away.

VI

Go away then, I tell them. Stop your whispering in shadows,
plucking at my scalp, sucking at my conscience.
Half-words almost heard,
how my hands are too soft and my thinking too,
how we've all gone soft.

They puzzle over the flushing of the loo.
Wonder why we waste the rich soil
they gave their lives to,
growing flowers that bear no fruit.

Lena, Ezekiel, Liza, Jebediah.
Names without faces, faces without names.

Go back to Georgia, Kentucky, Tennessee, Maryland,
Virginia, up on over the border to Pennsylvania.
Go back over to the side you should have fought on.
Change the colour of your uniform,
change your vote, change the fate, un-buy those slaves,
uncrack the cowhide, unlick your lips, that hunger
you have for black skin to lash, your tongue a weapon,
quoting the Good Book, washing your hands clean in holy water.

Leave the land to the Natives who know how to honour it.
Get back on that ship to England,
cross the channel back to France.
Take the Master out of Mister. Take off the H
you added to the family name. Return to your mother-tongue,
parlez vous again in the city you came from,
before they chased you out, or the grass got greener,
before the drought, the flood,
before some great great named John
went down with the ship called Increase,
before the long bitter of it all got passed down,
before the going down to the frozen ground
of the one without a name.

Call her Peace and let her rest. Amen.

Kate Bingham

Monogamy

SESTINA

I blame it on the backlash: free love
in the Eighties was for hippies, no one
liked Thatcher but monogamy
seemed more efficient, comforting to State
and individual alike, less last
resort than a celebration in bed

of the right to choose, not make your bed
and lie in it so much as a labour of love
we willingly fell in with, certain at last:
I wanted you, you wanted me. Alone
for the first time and in no fit state
for company we didn't see monogamy –

dumb, satisfied, unsung monogamy –
sneak in and slide between us on the bed,
backdating itself as if to reinstate
respectability, disguised as love's
romantic ideal and mocking our offhand, one
night stand bravado. It wants us to last,

our happiness, like a disease, its last
chance to spread – as if monogamy
transmits non-sexually from one
adoring couple to the next – to embed
itself in a world where pleasure and love
live separately and sit again in state,

pass sentence on what neither Church nor State
condemn outright. But what if we do last?
Time's not the test. Who loves best won't always love
longest, might not respect monogamy's
insistence, its assumption that all beds
must be forsaken but the one

one lies in in love. My eyes are for no one
but you, my love. We lie in a state
of easy innocence, a bed
of roses, tumbled and fragrant to the last
linen bud, but what's monogamy
without temptation, faith without love?

Therefore for love we should sacrifice one
thing alone: monogamy; maintain a state
of mutual jealousy, outlast our bed.

Eavan Boland

I have been wondering
what I have to leave behind, to give my daughters.

No good offering the view
between here and Three Rock Mountain,
the blueness in the hours before rain, the long haze afterwards.
The ground I stood on was never really mine. It might not ever
                                        be theirs.

And gifts that were passed through generations –
silver and the fluid light left after silk – were never given here.

This is an island of waters, inland distances,
with a history of want and women who struggled
to make the nothing which was all they had
into something they could leave behind.

I learned so little from them: the lace bobbin with its braided mesh,
its oat-straw pillow and the wheat-coloured shawl
knitted in one season
to imitate another

are all crafts I never had
and can never hand on. But then again there was a night
I stayed awake, alert and afraid, with my first child
who turned and turned; sick, fretful.

When dawn came I held my hand over the absence of fever,
over skin which had stopped burning, as if I knew the secrets
of health and air, as if I understood them

and listened to the silence
and thought, I must have learned that somewhere.

Sue Boyle

A Leisure Centre Is Also a Temple of Learning

The honey coloured girl in the women's changing room
is absorbed in making her body more beautiful:
she has flexed and toned every muscle with a morning swim
and showered away the pool chemicals
using an aromatic scrub and a gentle exfoliant.

Lithe as a young leopard, she has perfect bone structure:
her secret cleft is shaved as neatly as a charlatan's moustache.

In dreamy abstractedness she moisturises then spray perfumes
every part that might be loved. Her long hands
move in rhythm like a weaver's at a loom –
tipped throat, underchin, the little kisspoints below her ears,
the nuzzle between her breasts, her willow thighs.
She brushes her hair so clean it looks like a waterfall.

A bee could sip her.
She is summer cream slipped over raspberries.
She is so much younger than the rest of us.

She should look around.

We twelve are the chorus:

we know what happens next.

Colette Bryce

Our boat was slow to reach Bethsaida; winds oppressed us,
fast and cold, our hands were blistered from the oars.
We'd done to death our songs and jokes, with miles
to go, when Jesus spoke:

he said he'd crouched upon the shore, alone, engaged
in silent prayer, when, looking down, he started –
saw his own image crouching there. And when he leant
and dipped his hand

he swore he felt the fingers touch, and as he rose
the image stood and, slowly, each put out a foot
and took a step, and where they met, the weight of one
annulled the other;

then how he'd moved across the lake, walked on the soles
of his liquid self, and he described how cool it felt
on his aching, dusty feet; the way he'd strode a steady
course to board the boat

where we now sat – mesmerized. He gestured out
towards the shore, along the lake, then to himself,
and asked us all to visualize, to open what he always
called our 'fettered minds'.

John Burnside

History

St Andrews: West Sands; September 2001

Today
      as we flew the kites
– the sand spinning off in ribbons along the beach
and that gasoline smell from Leuchars gusting across
the golf links;
                the tide far out
and quail-grey in the distance;
                        people
jogging, or stopping to watch
as the war planes cambered and turned
in the morning light –

today
      – with the news in my mind, and the muffled dread
of what may come –

                I knelt down in the sand
with Lucas
          gathering shells
and pebbles
          finding evidence of life in all this
driftwork:
          snail shells; shreds of razorfish;
smudges of weed and flesh on tideworn stone.

At times I think what makes us who we are
is neither kinship nor our given states
but something lost between the world we own
and what we dream about behind the names

on days like this
                    our lines raised in the wind
our bodies fixed and anchored to the shore

and though we are confined by property
what tethers us to gravity and light
has most to do with distance and the shapes
we find in water
                    reading from the book
of silt and tides
                    the rose or petrol blue
of jellyfish and sea anemone
combining with a child's
first nakedness.

Sometimes I am dizzy with the fear
of losing everything – the sea, the sky,
all living creatures, forests, estuaries:
we trade so much to know the virtual
we scarcely register the drift and tug
of other bodies
                    scarcely apprehend
the moment as it happens: shifts of light
and weather
                    and the quiet, local forms
of history: the fish lodged in the tide
beyond the sands;
                    the long insomnia
of ornamental carp in public parks
captive and bright
                    and hung in their own
slow-burning
                    transitive gold;
                              jamjars of spawn
and sticklebacks
                    or goldfish carried home

from fairgrounds
                    to the hum of radio

but this is the problem: how to be alive
in all this gazed-upon and cherished world
and do no harm

                  a toddler on a beach
sifting wood and dried weed from the sand
and puzzled by the pattern on a shell

his parents on the dune slacks with a kite
plugged into the sky
                    all nerve and line

patient; afraid; but still, through everything
attentive to the irredeemable.

Matthew Caley

Lines Written Upon a Prophylactic Found
in a Brixton Gutter

O useless balloon, supine, not the colour of dolor
but see-thru, salmon-pink, plugged with your load of ore
draped in the grating side by side
with imploded pizza-stars and half a crepe.

Squished jellyfish of desire, trodden under the fly-boy trainers
of crack-dealers by the Taxi-rank and noodle-bar
– witness to a union of souls or alleyway tremble –
spermicidal eel, you know the perfidious trade-routes,

how the underground waters of the Effra
distabilise our feet, how pomegranate or melon-seeds
from the glass-arcades stuck in the tread of our boots

might spring up a rash of fruit trees in the inner city
sometime and knowing also how joy is brief [and rarely
                                    sanctioned by the Pontiff]
you dangle-drop, precariously, swim out for the open sea.

Ciaran Carson

THE WAR CORRESPONDENT

I
Gallipoli

Take sheds and stalls from Billingsgate,
glittering with scaling-knives and fish,
the tumbledown outhouses of English farmers' yards
that reek of dung and straw, and horses
cantering the mewsy lanes of Dublin;

take an Irish landlord's ruinous estate,
elaborate pagodas from a Chinese Delftware dish
where fishes fly through shrouds and sails and yards
of leaking ballast-laden junks bound for Benares
in search of bucket-loads of tea as black as tin;

take a dirty gutter from a back street in Boulogne,
where shops and houses teeter so their pitched roofs meet,
some chimney stacks as tall as those in Sheffield
or Irish round towers,
smoking like a fleet of British ironclad destroyers;

take the garlic-oregano-tainted arcades of Bologna,
linguini-twists of souks and smells of rotten meat,
as labyrinthine as the rifle-factories of Springfield,
or the tenements deployed by bad employers
who sit in parlours doing business drinking *Power's*;

then populate this slum with Cypriot and Turk,
Armenians and Arabs, British riflemen
and French Zouaves, camel-drivers, officers, and sailors,
sappers, miners, Nubian slaves, Greek money-changers,
plus interpreters who do not know the lingo;

dress them in turbans, shawls of fancy needlework,
fedoras, fezzes, sashes, shirts of fine Valenciennes,
boleros, pantaloons designed by jobbing tailors,
knickerbockers of the ostrich and the pink flamingo,
sans-culottes, and outfits even stranger;

requisition slaughter-houses for the troops,
and stalls with sherbet, lemonade, and rancid lard for sale,
a temporary hospital or two, a jail,
a stagnant harbour redolent with cholera,
and open sewers running down the streets;

let the staple diet be green cantaloupes
swarming with flies washed down with sour wine,
accompanied by the Byzantine
jangly music of the cithara
and the multi-lingual squawks of parakeets –

O landscape riddled with the diamond mines of Kimberley,
and all the oubliettes of Trebizond,
where opium-smokers doze among the Persian rugs,
and spies and whores in dim-lit snugs
discuss the failing prowess of the Allied powers,

where prowling dogs sniff for offal beyond
the stench of pulped plums and apricots,
from which is distilled the brandy they call 'grape-shot',
and soldiers lie dead or drunk among the crushed flowers –
I have not even begun to describe Gallipoli.

4
Balaklava

The Turks marched in dense columns, bristling with steel.
Sunlight flashed on the polished barrels of their firelocks
and on their bayonets, relieving their sombre hue,
for their dark blue uniforms looked quite black
when viewed *en masse*. The Chasseurs d'Afrique,
in light powder-blue jackets, with white cartouche belts, scarlet
pantaloons, mounted on white Arabs, caught the eye
like a bed of flowers scattered over the valley floor.

Some, indeed, wore poppies red as cochineal,
plucked from the rich soil, which bore an abundance of
    hollyhocks,
dahlias, anemones, wild parsley, mint, whitethorn, rue,
sage, thyme, and countless other plants whose names I lack.
As the Turkish infantry advanced, their boots creaked
and crushed the springy flowers, and delicate
perfumes wafted into the air beneath the April sky:
the smell of sweating men and horses smothered by flora.

Waving high above the more natural green
of the meadow were phalanxes of rank grass, marking the
    mounds
where the slain of October 25th had found their last repose,
and the snorting horses refused to eat those deadly shoots.
As the force moved on, more evidences of that fatal day
came to light. The skeleton of an English horseman
had tatters of scarlet cloth hanging to the bones of his arms;
all the buttons had been cut off the jacket.

Round as shot, the bullet-skull had been picked clean
save for two swatches of red hair. The remains of a wolfhound
sprawled at his feet. From many graves, the uncovered bones
of the tenants had started up, all of them lacking boots.

Tangled with rotted trappings, half-decayed horses lay
where they'd fallen. Fifes and drums struck up a rataplan;
so we swept on over our fellow men-at-arms
under the noon sun in our buttoned-up jackets.

Kate Clanchy

ONE, TWO

The camera has caught me
in a church doorway, stooping
to fasten what must be

my old cork-soled sandals,
their thick suede straps,
that dry, worn grip at heel

and instep. I'm smiling
downwards, pinkly
self-conscious, and above me

the arch is an extraordinary
blue. New – the whole place
was just lime-washed, azure

and sapphire rough-brushed
over moss. It stood in the moist heat
at a confluence of rivers –

I've even noted their names,
and the date, which says you, love,
are perhaps ten cells old.

In the humid space beneath
my dress, my body is bent
in the small effort of buckling,

the sag of my stomach briefly
leant on my thigh,
and, at the crux, in the press

of my nerveless places, you
are putting me on, easily,
the way a foot puts on a shoe.

Chris Considine

THE CRUELLEST CLASS

Roofed by drizzling cloud, sheep in their sections
await their turn for judgment.

First the tall sheep: curled Teeswaters,
Bluefaced Leicesters with imperial profiles.

Spotted and spiky Jacobs proud of their lineage,
Dalesbred and Swaledales and thug-faced Texels.

Each breed has its class and peculiar
classicism, its points and pedigree.

But here at the end is a motley group
lumped together as Butchers' Lambs,

some blackheaded, some white,
some randomly speckled, slumped,

most of them, on the smirched grass
as if aware of inferiority,

moving their jaws like sullen teenagers.
This one is listlessly nibbling

the blue twine that keeps him penned
fast. Only the smallest one

cries constantly, a bleak complaint
that splits his jaw, shivers the thin grey tongue.

But even these are washed and prinked,
creamy fleeces fluffed up and faces gleaming.

Stars today and meat tomorrow.

Wendy Cope

BEING BORING

> *'May you live in interesting times.'*
>   Chinese curse

If you ask me 'What's new?', I have nothing to say
Except that the garden is growing.
I had a slight cold but it's better today.
I'm content with the way things are going.
Yes, he is the same as he usually is,
Still eating and sleeping and snoring.
I get on with my work. He gets on with his.
I know this is all very boring.

There was drama enough in my turbulent past:
Tears and passion – I've used up a tankful.
No news is good news, and long may it last.
If nothing much happens, I'm thankful.
A happier cabbage you never did see,
My vegetable spirits are soaring.
If you're after excitement, steer well clear of me.
I want to go on being boring.

I don't go to parties. Well, what are they for,
If you don't need to find a new lover?
You drink and you listen and drink a bit more
And you take the next day to recover.
Someone to stay home with was all my desire
And, now that I've found a safe mooring,
I've just one ambition in life: I aspire
To go on and on being boring.

Julia Copus

An Easy Passage

Once she is halfway up there, crouched in her bikini
on the porch roof of her family's house, trembling,
she knows that the one thing she must not do is to think
of the narrow windowsill, the sharp
drop of the stairwell; she must keep her mind
on the friend with whom she is half in love
and who is waiting for her on the blond
gravel somewhere beneath her, keep her mind
on her and on the fact of the open window,
the flimsy, hole-punched, aluminium lever
towards which in a moment she will reach
with the length of her whole body, leaning in
to the warm flank of the house. But first she
steadies herself, still crouching, the grains of the asphalt
hot beneath her toes and fingertips,
a square of petrified beach. Her tiny breasts
rest lightly on her thighs. – What can she know
of the way the world admits us less and less
the more we grow? For now both girls seem
lit, as if from within, their hair and the gold stud
earrings in the first one's ears; for now the house exists
only for them, set back as it is from the long, grey
eye of the street, and far away from the mother
who does not trust her daughter with a key,
the workers about their business in the drab
electroplating factory over the road,
far too, most far, from the flush-faced secretary
who, with her head full of the evening class
she plans to take, or the trip of a lifetime, looks up now
from the stirring omens of the astrology column
at a girl – thirteen if she's a day – standing
in next to nothing in the driveway opposite,
one hand flat against her stomach, one

shielding her eyes to gaze up at a pale calf,
a silver anklet and the five neat *shimmering-oyster*-painted toenails of an outstretched foot
which catch the sunlight briefly like the
flash of armaments before
dropping gracefully into the shade of the house.

Allan Crosbie

Our patience will not yield, our resolve will not break.
We will liberate our children's minds.
We will protect their innocent hearts.
Our strong actions will follow our strong words.
The thirsty will drink, the hungry will eat.
We will teach you to believe what you read.

We will teach you to believe what you read.
Our patience will not yield, our resolve will not break.
The thirsty will drink, the hungry will eat.
We will liberate our children's minds.
Our strong actions will follow our strong words.
We will protect their innocent hearts.

We will protect your innocent hearts.
You will learn to believe what you read.
Strong actions will follow these strong words.
Our patience will not yield, our resolve will not break.
We will liberate our children's minds.
The thirsty will drink, the hungry will eat.

The hungry are drunk, the thirsty may eat.
We will not betray their innocent hearts.
We will not enslave our children's minds.
They will never disbelieve what they read.
Our patience will not yield, our resolve will not break.
Strong actions first demand strong words.

Strong actions first demand strong words
like, *If the thirsty drink and the hungry eat*
our patience will not yield, our resolve will not break.
We will not betray the innocent heart
of this manifesto – believe what you read.
Read my lips: we will enslave your children's minds.

To free them, we must enslave your children's minds.
The actions of the strong speak louder than their words –
if you refuse to believe what you read,
the thirsty won't drink, the hungry won't eat.
We will protect our innocent hearts.
We have patience. You will suffer, yield, break.

We will read your hungry minds.
We will break your strong, strong hearts.
You will eat our innocent words.

John F Deane

I too have gone down into my underworld
    seeking my father, as he went down into his;
we go on believing there is the possibility
    of discovering the rich knowledge that is held

like a life in amber and that we can return
    certain of what business we should be about. Here
is the very edge of dream, this the marsh, a green miasma
    hovering above; small birds, motionless, cling

to the reeds, like terror-stricken souls. You must cross
    in your journey, broad rivers spanned
by magnificent structures; you must cross, too,
    the laboured hills of Aquitaine and the neat

villages of Picardy. Great trucks go rushing by
    to somewhere that will not concern you; you pass
cherry trees by the roadside with their blood
    fruits, leave behind you

château, auberge, the diminished whisperings
    of wars; you will pass, too, fields of sunflowers,
those astonished and childish faces lifted
    in congregation. At a great distance the rough-cast

white of the highest mountains will appear at evening
    tipped with baby-pink; folk-art in medieval hill-top chapels
will draw out tears of innocence; in the baroque theatricals
    of later overwhelming churches, ghastly saints

will be sitting in their skeletal remains, grinning from glass caskets
  like dowdy stuffed birds; they shall remain for ever silent
and joyful on their couches. When you emerge, shaken, and carrying
  the ever-heavier burden of yourself, you may seek

solace in words, for the world burns to know what news
  the deepest darkness holds, but oh how you find
the words themselves pallid and languorous, so shy
  they lurk in hidden places like the most secretive

night animals. You will survive, you know, only as long
  as you hold to the narrow footpath, speaking your father's name
as if it served as talisman and wondering, when their time comes,
  will your children too go down into their underworld, seeking.

Tishani Doshi

THE DELIVERER

Our Lady of the Light Convent, Kerala

The sister here is telling my mother
How she came to collect children
Because they were crippled or dark or girls.

Found naked in the streets,
Covered in garbage, stuffed in bags,
Abandoned at their doorstep.

One of them was dug up by a dog,
Thinking the head barely poking above the ground
Was bone or wood, something to chew.

This is the one my mother will bring.

*

Milwaukee Airport, USA

The parents wait at the gates.
They are American so they know about ceremony
And tradition, about doing things right.

They haven't seen or touched her yet.
Don't know of her fetish for plucking hair off hands,
Or how her mother tried to bury her.

But they are crying.
We couldn't stop crying, my mother said,
Feeling the strangeness of her empty arms.

*

This girl grows up on video tapes,
Sees how she's passed from woman
To woman. She returns to twilight corners.

To the day of her birth,
How it happens in some desolate hut
Outside village boundaries

Where mothers go to squeeze out life,
Watch body slither out from body,

Feel for penis or no penis,
Toss the baby to the heap of others,

Trudge home to lie down for their men again.

Nick Drake

c/o the Sea at Patea

(in memory of Paul Winstanley)

I'd guess you thought of your life as a book
Of short stories, unpublished, their integrity
Ghosted by the rejection letters you kept
And replied to; or so I believe, who figured
In the months we coincided in the Alpujarras;
You in a derelict mill, in the one deckchair
Placed at the edge of a doorway into air
And evening light, the steps long gone, below
God's handful of scattered river rocks,
The river always awol but for the glints
Of currents in the silver of the stones;
In the distance, balanced terraces
Of oranges, olives, and white villages –
Almost, perhaps, an image of your ideal
Of a good life for all; food, land, dignity,
The kind of thing we'd drink to – I was young,
You were wiser – in the local wine
Rough as the tire-treads of our hippy sandals.
Then with your habitual economy
You packed yourself, your books, stones, recipes,
And hundreds of tapes into the old green tin
Of the favoured 2CV, and moved on again…
After a few letters we lost touch –
Until your memorial, and here you are
In photographs as everybody knew you;
Bald, bespectacled, moustached, that careful smile,
Like a comic we knew better than to name;
Lover of music, and bacon; detester of tissues;
And all the other stories I didn't know;
Pink Floyd roadie, potter, furniture maker,
Greenpeace engineer, political letter-writer;

'A life,' as you once wrote, 'seen as a whole –
As much as there was ever going to be.'
And finally here's the fisherman with his trophies
In the soft fawn cowboy hat now laid to rest
Beneath the cuttings of the local man
Who died, fishing, on New Year's Day. My dear,
(As you would say) I know it's far too late
To write a letter of any kind but this,
But I must, if only to stamp and post
With its best wishes and conditionals,
To Paul Winstanley c/o the Sea at Patea,
Your final and unchanging home address.

Carol Ann Duffy

The Map-Woman

A woman's skin was a map of the town
where she'd grown from a child.
When she went out, she covered it up
with a dress, with a shawl, with a hat,
with mitts or a muff, with leggings, trousers
or jeans, with an ankle-length cloak, hooded
and fingertip-sleeved. But – birthmark, tattoo –
the A-Z street-map grew, a precise second skin,
broad if she binged, thin when she slimmed,
a precis of where to end or go back or begin.

Over her breast was the heart of the town,
from the Market Square to the Picture House
by way of St Mary's Church, a triangle
of alleys and streets and walks, her veins
like shadows below the lines of the map, the river
an artery snaking north to her neck. She knew
if you crossed the bridge at her nipple, took a left
and a right, you would come to the graves,
the grey-haired teachers of English and History,
the soldier boys, the Mayors and Councillors,

the beloved mothers and wives, the nuns and priests,
their bodies fading into the earth like old print
on a page. You could sit on a wooden bench
as a wedding pair ran, ringed, from the church,
confetti skittering over the marble stones,
the big bell hammering hail from the sky, and wonder
who you would marry and how and where and when
you would die; or find yourself in the coffee house
nearby, waiting for time to start, your tiny face
trapped in the window's bottle-thick glass like a fly.

And who might you see, short-cutting through
the Grove to the Square – that line there, the edge
of a fingernail pressed on her flesh – in the rain,
leaving your empty cup, to hurry on after
calling their name? When she showered, the map
gleamed on her skin, blue-black ink from a nib.
She knew you could scoot down Greengate Street,
huddling close to the High House, the sensible shops,
the Swan Hotel, till you came to the Picture House,
sat in the musty dark watching the Beatles

run for a train or Dustin Hoffman screaming
Elaine! Elaine! Elaine! or the spacemen in 2001
floating to Strauss. She sponged, soaped, scrubbed;
the prison and hospital stamped on her back,
the park neat on her belly, her navel marking the spot
where the empty bandstand stood, the river again,
heading south, clear as an operation scar,
the war memorial facing the railway station
where trains sighed on the platforms, pining
for Glasgow, London, Liverpool. She knew

you could stand on the railway bridge, waving
goodbye to strangers who stared as you vanished
into the belching steam, tasting future time
on the tip of your tongue. She knew you could run
the back way home – there it was on her thigh –
taking the southern road then cutting off to the left,
the big houses anchored behind their calm green lawns,
the jewels of conkers falling down at your feet,
then duck and dive down Nelson and Churchill
and Kipling and Milton Way until you were home.

She didn't live there now. She lived down south,
abroad, en route, up north, on a plane or train
or boat, on the road, in hotels, in the back of cabs,
on the phone; but the map was under her stockings,

under her gloves, under the soft silk scarf at her throat,
under her chiffon veil, a delicate braille. Her left knee
marked the grid of her own estate. When she knelt
she felt her father's house pressing into the bone,
heard in her head the looped soundtrack of then –
a tennis ball repeatedly thumping a wall,

an ice-cream van crying and hurrying on, a snarl
of children's shrieks from the overgrown land
where the houses ran out. The motorway groaned
just out of sight. She knew you could hitch
from Junction 13 and knew of a girl who had not
been seen since she did; had heard of a kid who'd run
across all six lanes for a dare before he was tossed
by a lorry into the air like a doll. But the motorway
was flowing away, was a roaring river of metal
and light, cheerio, au revoir, auf wiedersehen, ciao.

She stared in the mirror as she got dressed,
both arms raised over her head, the roads
for east and west running from shoulder
to wrist, the fuzz of woodland or countryside under
each arm. Only her face was clear, her fingers
smoothing in cream, her baby-blue eyes unsure
as they looked at themselves. But her body was certain,
an inch to the mile, knew every nook and cranny,
cul-de-sac, stile, back road, high road, low road,
one-way street of her past. There it all was, back

to front in the glass. She piled on linen, satin, silk,
leather, wool, perfume and mousse and went out.
She got in a limousine. The map perspired
under her clothes. She took a plane. The map seethed
on her flesh. She spoke in a foreign tongue.
The map translated everything back to herself.
She turned out the light and a lover's hands
caressed the map in the dark from north to south,

lost tourists wandering here and there, all fingers
and thumbs, as their map flapped in the breeze.

So one day, wondering where to go next,
she went back, drove a car for a night and a day,
till the town appeared on her left, the stale cake
of the castle crumbled up on the hill; and she hired
a room with a view and soaked in the bath.
When it grew dark, she went out, thinking
she knew the place like the back of her hand,
but something was wrong. She got lost in arcades,
in streets with new names, in precincts
and walkways, and found that what was familiar

was only facade. Back in her hotel room, she stripped
and lay on the bed. As she slept, her skin sloughed
like a snake's, the skin of her legs like stockings, silvery,
sheer, like the long gloves of the skin of her arms,
the papery camisole from her chest a perfect match
for the tissuey socks of the skin of her feet. Her sleep
peeled her, lifted a honeymoon thong from her groin,
a delicate bra of skin from her breasts, and all of it
patterned A to Z; a small cross where her parents' skulls
grinned at the dark. Her new skin showed barely a mark.

She woke and spread out the map on the floor. What
was she looking for? Her skin was her own small ghost,
a shroud to be dead in, a newspaper for old news
to be read in, gift-wrapping, litter, a suicide letter.
She left it there, dressed, checked out, got in the car.
As she drove, the town in the morning sun glittered
behind her. She ate up the miles. Her skin itched,
like a rash, like a slow burn, felt stretched, as though
it belonged to someone else. Deep in the bone
old streets tunnelled and burrowed, hunting for home.

Ian Duhig

After the fair, I'd still a light heart
And a heavy purse, he struck so cheap.
And cattle doted on him: in his time
Mine only dropped heifers, fat as cream.
Yields doubled. I grew fond of company
That knew when to shut up. Then one night,

Disturbed from dreams of my dear late wife,
I hunted down her torn voice to his pale form.
Stock-still in the light from the dark lantern,
Stark-naked but for the fox-trap biting his ankle,
I knew him a warlock, a cow with leather horns.
To go into the hare gets you muckle sorrow,

The wisdom runs, muckle care. I levelled
And blew the small hour through his heart.
The moon came out. By its yellow witness
I saw him fur over like a stone mossing.
His lovely head thinned. His top lip gathered.
His eyes rose like bread. I carried him

In a sack that grew lighter at every step
And dropped him from a bridge. There was no
Splash. Now my herd's elf-shot. I don't dream
But spend my nights casting ball from half-crowns
And my days here. Bless me, Father, I have sinned.
It has been an hour since my last confession.

Helen Dunmore

To My Nine-Year-Old Self

You must forgive me. Don't look so surprised,
perplexed, and eager to be gone,
balancing on your hands or on the tightrope.
You would rather run than walk, rather climb than run
rather leap from a height than anything.

I have spoiled this body we once shared.
Look at the scars, and watch the way I move,
careful of a bad back or a bruised foot.
Do you remember how, three minutes after waking
we'd jump straight out of the ground floor window
into the summer morning?

That dream we had, no doubt it's as fresh in your mind
as the white paper to write it on.
We made a start, but something else came up –
a baby vole, or a bag of sherbet lemons –
and besides, that summer of ambition
created an ice-lolly factory, a wasp trap
and a den by the cesspit.

I'd like to say that we could be friends
but the truth is we have nothing in common
beyond a few shared years. I won't keep you then.
Time to pick rosehips for tuppence a pound,
time to hide down scared lanes
from men in cars after girl-children,

or to lunge out over the water
on a rope that swings from that tree
long buried in housing –
but no, I shan't cloud your morning. God knows
I have fears enough for us both –

I leave you in an ecstasy of concentration
slowly peeling a ripe scab from your knee
to taste it on your tongue.

Douglas Dunn

THE YEAR'S AFTERNOON

As the moment of leisure grows deeper
I feel myself sink like a slow root
Into the herbaceous lordship of my place.
This is my time, my possessive, opulent
Freedom in free-fall from salaried routines,
Intrusions, the boundaryless tedium.
This is my liberty among trees and grass
When silence is the mind's imperfect ore
And a thought turns and dallies in its space
Unhindered by desire or transactions.
For three hours without history or thirst
Time is my own unpurchased and intimate
Republic of the cool wind and blue sea.
For three hours I shall be my own tutor
In the coastal hedge-school of grass furniture.
Imaginary books fly to my hand
From library trees. They are all I need.
Birdsong is a chirp of meditative silence
Rendered in fluttered boughs, and I am still,
Very still, in philosophical light.
I am all ears in my waterside aviary.
My breath is poised for truth to whisper from
Inner invisibilities and the holiness
Venturesome little birds live with always
In their instinctive comforts. I am shedding
The appetites of small poetry and open to
Whatever visits me. I am all eyes
When light moves on water and the leaves shake.
I am very still, a hedge-hidden sniper
In whose sights clarified infinity sits
Smiling at me, and my skin is alive
To thousands of brushed touches, very light
Delicate kisses of time, thought kisses,

Touches which have come out of hiding shyly
Then go back again into the far away
Surrender they came from and where they live.
Perfecting my afternoon, I am alert to
Archival fragrances that float to me
Unexplained over the world's distances.
This is my time. I am making it real.
I am getting rid of myself. This is my time.
I am free to do whatever I wish
In these hours, and I have chosen this
Liberty, which is an evanishment
To the edges of breath, a momentary
Loss of the dutiful, a destitute
Perchance, a slipping away from life's
Indignities and works into my freedom
Which is beyond all others and is me.
I am free to do as I like, and do this;
I sink like a slow root in the name of life
And in the name of what it is I do.
These are my hours of 1993.
Ears, eyes, nose, skin and taste have gone.
For a little while I shall be nothing and good.
Then other time will come back, and history.
I shall get up and leave my hiding place,
My instinctive, field-sized republic.
I shall go home, and be that other man.
I shall go to my office. I shall live
Another year longing for my hours
In the complete afternoon of sun and salt.
My empty shoes at the bedside will say to me,
'When are we taking you back?' Why be patient?
You have much more, so much more, to lose.'

Paul Durcan

The Far Side of the Island

Driving over the mountain to the far side of the island
I am brooding neither on what lies ahead of me
Nor on what lies behind me. Up here
On top of the mountain, in the palm of its plateau,
I am being contained by its wrist and its fingertips.

The middle of the journey is what is at stake –
Those twenty-five miles or so of in-betweenness
In which marrow of mortality hardens
In the bones of the nomad. From finite end
To finite end, the orthopaedics of mortality.

Up here on the plateau above the clouds,
Peering down on the clouds in the valleys,
There are no fences, only moorlands
With wildflowers as far as the eye can see;
The earth's unconscious in its own pathology.

Yet when I arrive at the far side of the island
And peer down at the outport on the rocks below,
The Atlantic Ocean rearing raw white knuckles,
Although I am globally sad I am locally glad
To be about to drive down that corkscrew road.

Climbing down the tree-line, past the first cottage,
Past the second cottage, behind every door
A neighbour. It is the company of his kind
Man was born for. Could I have known,
Had I not chanced the far side of the island?

UA Fanthorpe

A MINOR ROLE

I'm best observed on stage,
Propping a spear, or making endless
Exits and entrances with my servant's patter,
Yes, sir. O no, sir. If I get
These midget moments wrong, the monstrous fabric
Shrinks to unwanted sniggers.

But my heart's in the unobtrusive,
The waiting-room roles: driving to hospitals,
Parking at hospitals. Holding hands under
Veteran magazines; making sense
Of consultants' monologues; asking pointed
Questions politely; checking dosages,
Dates; getting on terms with receptionists;
Sustaining the background music of civility.

At home in the street you may see me
Walking fast in case anyone stops:
O, getting on, getting better my formula
For well-meant intrusiveness.
                              At home,
Thinking ahead: *Bed? A good idea!*
(Bed solves a lot); answer the phone,
Be wary what I say to it, but grateful always;
Contrive meals for a hunger-striker; track down
Whimsical soft-centred happy-all-the-way-through novels;
Find the cat (mysteriously reassuring);
Cancel things, tidy things; pretend all's well,
Admit it's not.

Learn to conjugate all the genres of misery:
Tears, torpor, boredom, lassitude, yearnings
For a simpler illness, like a broken leg.

Enduring ceremonial delays. Being referred
Somewhere else. Consultant's holiday. Saying *Thank you*
For anything to everyone
                            Not the star part.
And who would want it? I jettison the spear,
The servant's tray, the terrible drone of Chorus:
Yet to my thinking this act was ill-advised
It would have been better to die*. No it wouldn't!

I am here to make you believe in life.

*Chorus: from *Oedipus Rex*, trans EF Watling

Helen Farish

She loves the radio, the freedom it gives
to listen out the back or as she's passing to and fro
or sitting in the half-house half-garden room

on a midsummer's Sunday evening
listening to a three-hour programme on the monsoon,
and the front door is open and the back,

and every now and then the setting light
coming past the lavender she's recently started caring for
and the honeysuckle she never used to notice nor those roses

hidden till she chopped back the buddleia – the light
coming past the flowering jasmine and the hanging basket
she's so pleased with stops her,

makes her see how much of her life
has been lived in this house,
that she's become who she is here

and what she will remember of these years is not
the times when living alone seemed a problem to solve
but the peace:

looking at a house she has done her best in,
loving small successes, the hanging basket, the picture in the half-
house half-garden room, that repotted plant,

and her larger successes – allowing herself the pleasure
of a three-hour programme on the monsoon
sorting through a box of postcards with a green glass of gin,

seeing all those places she's been to: but her journey
to this programme, her swept front path, this is
the one she's most proud of.

Paul Farley

Shorter than the blink inside a blink
the National Grid will sometimes make, when you'll
turn to a room and say: *Was that just me?*

People sitting down for dinner don't feel
their chairs taken away / put back again
much faster than that trick with tablecloths.

A train entering the Olive Mount cutting
shudders, but not a single passenger
complains when it pulls in almost on time.

The birds feel it, though, and if you see
starlings in shoal, seagulls abandoning
cathedral ledges, or a mob of pigeons

lifting from a square as at gunfire,
be warned, it may be happening, but then
those sensitive to bat-squeak in the backs

of necks, who claim to hear the distant roar
of comets on the turn – these may well smile
at a world restored, in one piece; though each place

where mineral Liverpool goes wouldn't believe
what hit it: all that sandstone out to sea
or meshed into the quarters of Cologne.

I've felt it a few times when I've gone home,
if anything, more often now I'm old,
and the gaps between get shorter all the time.

Vicki Feaver

The Gun

Bringing a gun into a house
changes it.

You lay it on the kitchen table,
stretched out like something dead
itself: the grainy polished wood stock
jutting over the edge,
the long metal barrel
casting a grey shadow
on the green-checked cloth.

At first it's just practice:
perforating tins
dangling on orange string
from trees in the garden.
Then a rabbit shot
clean through the head.

Soon the fridge fills with creatures
that have run and flown.
Your hands reek of gun oil
and entrails. You trample
fur and feathers. There's a spring
in your step; your eyes gleam
like when sex was fresh.

A gun brings a house alive.

I join in the cooking: jointing
and slicing, stirring and tasting –
excited as if the King of Death
had arrived to feast, stalking
out of winter woods,
his black mouth
sprouting golden crocuses.

Leontia Flynn

Like many folk, when first I saddled a rucksack,
feeling its weight on my back –
the way my spine
curved under it like a meridian –

I thought: Yes. This is how
to live. On the beaten track, the sherpa pass, between
  Krakow
and Zagreb, or the Siberian white
cells of scattered airports,

it came clear as over a tannoy
that in restlessness, in anony
mity:
was some kind of destiny.

So whether it was the scare stories about Larium
– the threats of delirium
and baldness – that led me, not to a Western Union
wiring money with six words of Lithuanian,

but to this post office with a handful of bills
or a giro; and why, if I'm stuffing smalls
hastily into a holdall, I am less likely
to be catching a Greyhound from Madison to
  Milwaukee

than to be doing some overdue laundry
is really beyond me.
However,
when, during routine evictions, I discover

alien pants, cinema stubs, the throwaway
comment – on a Post-it – or a tiny stowaway
pressed flower amid bottom drawers,
I know these are my souvenirs

and, from these crushed valentines, this unravelled
sports sock, that the furthest distances I've travelled
have been those between people. And what survives
of holidaying briefly in their lives.

Roderick Ford

GIUSEPPE

My Uncle Giuseppe told me
that in Sicily in World War Two,
in the courtyard behind the aquarium,
where the bougainvillea grows so well,
the only captive mermaid in the world
was butchered on the dry and dusty ground
by a doctor, a fishmonger, and certain others.

She, it, had never learned to speak
because she was simple, or so they'd said.
But the priest who held one of her hands
while her throat was cut,
said she was only a fish, and fish can't speak.
But she screamed like a woman in terrible fear.

And when they took a ripe golden roe
from her side, the doctor said
this was proof she was just a fish
and anyway an egg is not a child,
but refused when some was offered to him.

Then they put her head and her hands
in a box for burial
and someone tried to take her wedding ring,
but the others stopped him,
and the ring stayed put.

The rest they cooked and fed to the troops.
They said a large fish had been found on the beach.

Starvation forgives men many things,
my uncle, the aquarium keeper, said,
but couldn't look me in the eye,
for which I thank God.

Linda France

Last night I dreamt of Delia Smith again –
smoked buckling simmering on the horizon,
that old Doverhouse moon stuffing the dumpling
of a crackling sky. She played en papillote

for just long enough to sweat me garlicky.
After I'd peppered her liver, stuffed her goose
and dogfished her tender loins, she was pâté
in my hands. She got all mulligatawny

so I tossed her into a nine herb salad
of Hintlesham. She was my Russian herring,
my giblet stock. We danced the ossobuco;
her belly kedgeree, her breasts prosciutto.

I tongue-casseroled her ear she was my Queen
of Puddings and wouldn't we sausage lots
of little quichelets, a platter of sprats
we'd name Béarnaise, Mortadella, Bara brith.

But when the trout hit the tabasco, it turned out
she was only pissaladière, garam
masala as a savoyard. Arrowroot.
Just another dip in love with crudités.

And I've stroganoffed with too many of them.
I chopped home to my own bloater paste and triped
myself into a carcass. No wonder I woke up
with scarlet farts, dried blood under my fingernails,

dreaming of Delia, her oxtail, again.

Tom French

NIGHT DRIVE

The closest, Mother, we have been in years
was a night drive back from Achill on our own.
Our tyres pressed their smooth cheeks to the ice,
gripping nothing, squealing, barely holding on.

Something stepped into our beam and stood there,
dumbly, ready to confront its death.
I remember your right hand in the darkness –
a white bird frightened from its fastness

in your lap, bracing yourself for the impact,
hearing you whisper '*Jesus*' under your breath,
preparing your soul for the moment of death.
Then, just as suddenly, nothing happened –

the sheep stepped back into the verge
for no reason, attracted by a clump of grass.
For days I felt the pressure of your hand on mine.
You would've led me to the next world, Mother, like a child.

John Fuller

My Life on the Margins of Celebrity

I sat on Beatrix Lehmann's knee, terrified that she was
    undead;

I saw Laurel and Hardy alive at the Lewisham Hippodrome,
    and they were gratified by my laughter;

I bowed to Queen Mary, widow of George V, in Greenwich
    Park, and from her limousine of midnight hue she
    nodded graciously back;

I was inspected in full uniform by Field-Marshal Montgomery:
    his cornflower-blue eyes passed within twenty inches
    of mine, and he departed in a bullet-proof car;

I sang for Vaughan Williams, his great head sunk on his
    waistcoat, neither awake nor asleep;

I watched Jonathan Miller lift a white mouse by its tail and
    drop it in a killing-bottle for me as an illustration of
    something or other;

I saw Frank Swift pick up a football with one hand;

I waited in the wings for my own entrance while Oliver
    Sacks played de Falla's 'Ritual Fire Dance' in a sash
    and a lurid spotlight;

I asked T. S. Eliot what he was writing, and his answer shall
    remain a secret;

I rang up the curtain on Dennis Potter in his first public
    performance, playing the part of a Romanian-French
    playwright;

I trod the throbbing boards of an ocean liner with Burt
      Lancaster, who was very small, and who smiled his
      characteristically delicate sneering smile;

I was asked to stay on in my first job, but politely declined
      and was succeeded in office by the Earl of Gowrie;

I drove Edward Albee to Niagara Falls, where he was silent
      among the thickly-iced trees;

I held Sam Mendes in my arms, but was more interested in
      his father's collection of Japanese pornography;

I brushed away cobwebs that had been sprayed on my hair
      by David Attenborough;

I played heads-bodies-and-legs with Henry Moore;

The Poet Laureate sent me reams of his verse, which I
      regretfully refused to publish;

I handed Debra Winger a glass of wine and did not tell her
      who I was;

I played against William Golding's French Defence and
      infiltrated my King's Knight to d6 and he couldn't
      avoid going a piece down;

And all this is true, and life is but a trail of dust between the
      stars;

The unremembered shall be forgotten, and the remembered
      also;

The dead shall be dead, and also the living.

Lydia Fulleylove

Night Drive

So when the phone call came, saying
    that we should go back tonight, we were barely
surprised, we might have been waiting
    for it all our lives. We took two cars in case
it did not happen that night and one of us
    at least could drive home to sleep and I
followed my father so as not to lose my way
    through the twisting lanes in the dark
but I think it was marked in my head
    and I would not have faltered even
though all the time I was thinking
    of my mother, the bones stretching
her beautiful skin and her left eye almost
    closed, her face as clear as the rear lights
of my father's car or the sign of the inn
    where we'd eaten that morning.
There was nothing to do but to keep on
    driving, the car flowing between the banks
until at last we were crossing the glare
    of the town to the place where my mother
lay dying, though perhaps not tonight,
    we knew that the end might not be tonight.

John Goodby

Uncles, talking the camshaft or the gimbal connected
to a slowly oscillating crank. The Uncles Brickell,
Swarfega kings, enseamed with swarf and scobs, skin
measled with gunmetal but glistening faintly, loud
in the smoke. Lithe and wiry above the lathe, milling out
a cylinder to a given bore. Uncles, pencil-stubs at their ears,
spurning ink, crossing sevens like émigré intellectuals,
measuring in thous and thirty-secondths (scrawled
on torn fag-packets); feinting with slide rules, racing,
but mild not as mild steel. Pockets congested, always. Uncles
with dockets for jobs, corners transparent with grease,
with a light machine oil. Time-served, my Uncles, branch-
ing out into doorhandles, grub-screws and the brass bits
that hold the front of the motor case to the rear flange
of the mounting panel. Release tab. Slightly hard of hearing
now, the Uncles, from the din of the shop, slowly nodding.
Uncles in 'Red Square'; uncles swapping tolerance gauges,
allen keys, telephone numbers, deals and rank commun-
ism. Forefingers describing arcs and cutting angles. White
and milky with coolants and lubricants, mess of order. Never
forgetting to ply a broom after. The missing half-finger, not
really missed any longer, just a banjo-hand gone west. My
Uncles still making a go of mower blades, on the road
at their age; offering cigars at Christmas. Uncanny if
encountered in visors, overalls, confounding nephews
in dignity of their calling, their epoch-stewed tea. Stand
a spoon in all their chamfered years, cut short or long. Uncles
immortal in the welding shed, under neon, lounge
as the vast doors slide to a cool blue dusk. My Uncles.

Vona Groarke

BODKIN

A word from a dream, or several, spiked on it
like old receipts. Something akin to a clavicle's
bold airs; a measurement of antique land;
a keepsake brooch on a quilted silk bodice;
a firkin, filled to the brink with mead or milk;
a bobbin spinning like a back-road drunken bumpkin;
borrowed, half-baked prophecies in a foreign tongue;
a debunked uncle's thin bloodline; a Balkan
fairy story, all broken bones poked inside out;
a bespoke book blacked in with Indian ink;
a bobolink in a buckeye or a bare-backed oak;
a barren spindle, choked ankle-high with lichen;
a fistful of ball bearings dropped on a *bodhrán*.
Body skin. Kith and kin. Other buckled things.

Paul Groves

My father used to get a six-inch nail,
position it above the little 'eye',
and give one hammer stroke. If all went well
he would not need another to gain entry
to the hidden heart. Maraca-like,

it had been shaken roughly near an ear.
Once I had heard that distant inner lake
it became time to taste its magic water.
The coconut smacked of an old ape's breast,
fibrous and alien. Spike extracted,

my father raised the fruit as if a blest
offering, and carefully enacted
the ancient ritual. I sampled next.
We changed to sucklings at a sacred pap.
No word was said. This went below all text

into a tribal memory. The sap
was drained, and then the butchery began.
The wooden ball was placed on a flat stone
and axed into two halves. He lifted one
and left the second portion, which was mine.

Jen Hadfield

This is how the catch is gutted –
you diddle the knife down fatty silver,
fingernail-deep, the broad blade's tip.
Slow burgundies stain the enamel sink.
Mackerel hoop and harden in your grip.
With tugsome bravery you yank
the gut-end, coda of a bloodless old song;
the silty fruits coddled away;
the clean fish and its swimbladder,
like a tigerlily,
                    on the cutting board

Michael Hamburger

The Dog-Days Interrupted

When in hottest July
Thunder rips the sky,
Blown grey clouds block the white,
Not quite burnt out a few red poppies loom
Among the fallen that wait
For after-life, prostrate,
Short showers too late
For all save the long-suffering to bloom,
Winds mix the season's light,
Mixed currents bring relief
To the still clinging leaf,
To fruit still filling, flower to come,
Myrtle moons budding in their darkness yet
And human sharer, grim
Before that interim.
But now the butterflies
From near-abeyance rise
Mingled, the early, late,
The commonest, the rare –
A feverish consummation
Almost too rich for buddleia-searching eyes.
This whitethroat, more inferred
Than either seen or heard,
Flits in to fit the word.
Thanks to the thunder only, winnowing,
A wane has mended, a clash has purged the air.

Sophie Hannah

GOD'S ELEVENTH RULE

I want to sit beside the pool all day,
Swim now and then, read *Peeping Tom*, a novel
By Howard Jacobson. You needn't pay
To hire a car to drive me to a hovel
Full of charred native art. Please can I stay
Behind? I will if necessary grovel.
I want to sit beside the pool all day,
Swim now and then, read *Peeping Tom*, a novel.

Pardon? You're worried I will find it boring?
My days will be repetitive and flat?
You think it would be oodles more alluring
To see the chair where Mao Tse Tung once sat.
Novels and pools are all I need for touring,
My *Peeping Tom*, *Nostromo* after that.
Pardon? You're worried I will find it boring.
My days will be repetitive and flat.

Okay, so you were right about *Nostromo*,
But I've a right to stay in this hotel.
Sienna: I refused to see *il duomo*.
(Does that mean Mussolini? Who can tell?)
In Spain I told them, 'Baño, bebo, como.'
I shunned the site where Moorish warriors fell.
Okay, so you were right about *Nostromo*
But I've a right to stay in this hotel.

I'm so alarmed, my voice becomes falsetto
When you prescribe a trip round local slums.
Would I drag you from Harvey Nicks to Netto?
No I would not. Down, down go both my thumbs.
I'm happy in this five-star rich man's ghetto
Where teeth are, by and large, attached to gums.

I'm so alarmed, my voice becomes falsetto
When you prescribe a trip round local slums.

It's not an English thing. No need to grapple
With the strange ways we foreigners behave.
My colleague would be thrilled to see your chapel,
Turrets and frescos and your deepest cave,
But as for me, I'd rather watch sun dapple
The contours of a chlorinated wave.
It's not an English thing. No need to grapple
With the strange ways we foreigners behave.

I want to spend all day beside the pool.
I wish that this were needless repetition,
But next to you, a steroid-guzzling mule,
A hunger strike and the first Christian mission
Look apathetic. God's eleventh rule:
Thou shalt get sore feet at an exhibition.
I want to spend all day beside the pool.
I wish that this were needless repetition.

David Harsent

STREET SCENES

(i)

Two greybeards playing chess, would you believe,
their sweetwood table and chairs at one remove
from the corner of the crossroads, where a dove
drifts down through the trompe l'oeil clouds of a gable-
   end to LOVE
IS ALL YOU NEED and SNAJPER! One grips his sleeve
to wipe his nose; one threatens the knight's move.
The same crossroads where push has so often come to
   shove.

(ii)

Broken glass in the Street of Clocks
Empty coats in the Street of Spindles
In the Street of Bridegrooms, broken locks
Burning books in the Street of Candles

(iii)

If you look closely you can see what it is, but you do have to look
closely, what with the early-evening light skating on the slick
and coming back at you off puddles on the tarmac.
This would have been three hours or more after the attack,
everything lying heavy, everything seeming to own the trick
of stillness, that shopping trolley, for instance, the gutted truck,
and these: one face-down over there, one in the crook
of another's arm, one flat out, one heaped like an open book,
one caught on the turn, arms out like a stopped clock,
one leaning against a door, as if about to knock.
But that over there: look again: did you ever see the like?

(iv)

The 'Golden Couple of Ballroom' are dancing the alley-ways,
soft-shoeing amid the shrapnel, lost in each other's gaze.

(v)

Something going through, something much like a hound
or wolf, in the hour *entre chien et loup*, the blue
hour when birdsong stops, just for a minute or two,
and the dead in the graveyard shuffle up the queue.

Something lean and low-slung, its muzzle to the ground,
something leaving a drip-trail of blood or piss.
It has come by way of the rift and the pretty pass,
slipping between the dead cert and the near-miss.

Something that whines and whimpers, much like the sound
of a child in pain, or love's last gasp. It shows
a backbone like a hat-rack, an eye like a bruise,
in its mouth, a rib (is it?), dark meat, the pope's nose.

Seamus Heaney

I

All of us came in Doctor Kerlin's bag.
He'd arrive with it, disappear to the room
And by the time he'd reappear to wash

Those nosy, rosy, big, soft hands of his
In the scullery basin, its lined insides
(The colour of a spaniel's inside lug)

Were empty for all to see, the trap-sprung mouth
Unsnibbed and gaping wide. Then like a hypnotist
Unwinding us, he'd wind the instruments

Back into their lining, tie the cloth
Like an apron round itself,
Darken the door and leave

With the bag in his hand, a plump ark by the keel...
Until the next time came and in he'd come
In his fur-lined collar that was also spaniel-coloured

And go stooping up to the room again, a whiff
Of disinfectant, a Dutch interior gleam
Of waistcoat satin and highlights on the forceps.

Getting the water ready, that was next –
Not plumping hot, and not lukewarm, but soft,
Sud-luscious, saved for him from the rain-butt

And savoured by him afterwards, all thanks
Denied as he towelled hard and fast,
Then held his arms out suddenly behind him

To be squired and silk-lined into the camel coat.
At which point he once turned his eyes upon me,
Hyperborean, beyond-the-north-wind blue,

Two peepholes to the locked room I saw into
Every time his name was mentioned, skimmed
Milk and ice, swabbed porcelain, the white

And chill of tiles, steel hooks, chrome surgery tools
And blood dreeps in the sawdust where it thickened
At the foot of each cold wall. And overhead

The little, pendent, teat-hued infant parts
Strung neatly from a line up near the ceiling –
A toe, a foot and shin, an arm, a cock

A bit like the rosebud in his buttonhole.

2

Poeta doctus Peter Levi says
Sanctuaries of Asclepius (called *asclepions*)
Were the equivalent of hospitals

In ancient Greece. Or of shrines like Lourdes,
Says *poeta doctus* Graves. Or of the cure
By poetry that cannot be coerced,

Say I, who realized at Epidaurus
That the whole place was a sanatorium
With theatre and gymnasium and baths,

A site of incubation, where 'incubation'
Was technical and ritual, meaning sleep
When epiphany occurred and you met the god…

Hatless, groggy, shadowing myself
As the thurifer I was in an open-air procession
In Lourdes in '56

When I nearly fainted from the heat and fumes,
Again I nearly fainted as I bent
To pull a bunch of grass and hallucinated

Doctor Kerlin at the steamed-up glass
Of the scullery window, starting in to draw
With his large pink index finger dot-faced men

With button-spots in a straight line down their fronts
And women with dot breasts, giving them all
A set of droopy sausage-arms and legs

That soon began to run. And then as he dipped and laved
In the generous suds again, *miraculum*:
The baby bits all came together swimming

Into his soapy big hygienic hands
And I myself came to, blinded with sweat,
Blinking and shaky in the windless light.

   3
Bits of the grass I pulled I posted off
To one going in to chemotherapy
And one who had come through. I didn't want

To leave the place or link up with the others.
It was midday, mid-May, pre-tourist sunlight
In the precincts of the god,

The very site of the temple of Asclepius.
I wanted nothing more than to lie down
Under hogweed, under seeded grass

And to be visited in the very eye of the day
By Hygeia, his daughter, her name still clarifying
The haven of light she was, the undarkening door.

4

The room I came from and the rest of us all came from
Stays pure reality where I stand alone,
Standing the passage of time, and she's asleep

In sheets put on for the doctor, wedding presents
That showed up again and again, bridal
And usual and useful at births and deaths.

Me at the bedside, incubating for real,
Peering, appearing to her as she closes
And opens her eyes, then lapses back

Into a faraway smile whose precinct of vision
I would enter every time, to assist and be asked
In that hoarsened whisper of triumph,

'And what do you think
Of the new wee baby the doctor brought for us all
When I was asleep?'

David Herd

SEPTEMBER 11TH, 2001

Worked in the morning.

Watched TV.

Ellen Hinsey

XVII
CORRESPONDENCES

APHORISMS REGARDING IMPATIENCE

1.
Mythologies of the End
Each century believing itself poised as if on the edge of time.

2.
The Meaning of Impatience
Restlessness in time. To imagine that which is not swiftly
accomplished will never be fulfilled.

3.
Displaced Envy
Unable to initiate creation, or manage civilization: the drive
to engineer *decreation* with perfection.

4.
Perplexing Instincts
The division of the spirit between advancement and
abandon.

5.
The Attraction of the Apocalypse
To control with absolute certainty one thing. And for it to
be the last.

6.
Fragile Vector
The intersection where civilization and perseverance meet.

7.
The Effort of Civilization
Miraculous labor. Each day Sisyphus rolling his rock uphill
against the accidental nature of mankind.

8.
Not a Solution
To draw into question Sisyphus's task.

9.
Accepting Negative Inevitability
Intellectual sleepwalking. The ethical self abdicating
affirmation for the temptation of *renunciation*.

10.
Deviant Logic
To reject contingencies of disaster. To glean *possibility* from
the crevices of *improbability*.

11.
What is at Stake
The fragile geometry of the world held in hostage.

12.
Not the End
A type of grace: waiting in impatience to see that, from now
until the far edge of always, *nothing happens*.

Mick Imlah

The Ayrshire Orpheus

And down he went, sounding the deepest floors
Where Pluto ruled with serious Proserpine,
Still piping, till he reached their double doors
And knocked. And so he saw her, horribly thin:
Eurydice, her face all eaten in,
Curled at the feet of that disdainful pair
Who feigned surprise to see a Scotsman there.

Then Orpheus, soft and urgent, half in dread
Of what she had become: 'My bonny lass –
Hey – love – though it's better than being dead –
What's happened to your lovely lips and face?
How have they disappeared, or come to this?'
And she: 'Shoosh, pet, right now I dare not say –
But you shall hear the whole another day',

As Pluto intervened: 'Your silly wife
Has marred her face, and turned her belly barren,
Through dwelling on the home she may not have;
Mindful of Ballantrae and the view of Arran,
She finds the mills of Hell friendless and foreign;
If one could spring her now to the Ayrshire coast,
No doubt her looks would heal to their uttermost!'

So Orpheus sat before that mocking twosome
And let them have it, with his matchless voice,
Pitching 'Ye Banks and Braes' at the royal bosom;
A charming 'Ae Fond Kiss', and 'Ca' the Yowes',
And then 'My love is like a red, red rose';
Till Pluto swooned, and prickly Proserpine
Lay down her softening form upon the green.

The infernal lakes had filled with lily water,
Such was the gentle power of that recital,
When Pluto cleared his throat: 'I thank the Scot
Who wrote these songs, and you, who made them vital;
Name your own prize, and that shall be requital.'
And Orpheus begged, 'Then let me take my love
Back to that place we owned in the world above.'

Which tickled Pluto. – 'You're a bold one, Mac!
– Yet I'm inclined to grant such a request,
On this condition: should you once *look back*,
Your wife reverts to Hell of the heaviest!'
Then Orpheus clasped her freshening to his chest,
And up they strove, spiralling in their fate,
Till they had almost reached the outward gate.

If you have loved, imagine the sweet chat
The two then had, rejoining their own kind –
So can you blame him, in the midst of that,
If he should suffer a local lapse of mind?
I hate to say – she fell a yard behind –
Backward he blinked – chains belted from the deeps
And yanked Eurydice to Hell for keeps.

Poor Orpheus! He felt like some old town
Of Carrick in decline: Maybole, or Girvan,
The pubs shut down, the kids, taunting 'the clown
Who couldna face the front', on drugs from Irvine;
While dismal in the twilight of surviving
Alone with his shopping, sore to be rid of her,
He walks the roads of home a widower.

AB Jackson

Oncology Centre. Cast-iron cabinets
of case histories, fresh figures, a request
in triplicate for a 'marrow harvest'...
I picture a bumpkin surgeon, in a sweat,
sorting cells like apples into buckets.

Facts are sensitive here. I work my way
through bales of personal files (always 'cancer'),
my throat cracked by so much dusty paper.
Truth comes to light on X-ray:

someone's brain, a wrinkled slice of fruit;
the skull's bone, a phosphorescent hoop,
classified and coded. Someone who.

Dear X, whatever daily face you wear,
may you never falter, never flower.

Kathleen Jamie

SPEIRIN

Binna feart, hinny,
yin day we'll gang thegither
tae thae stourie
blaebellwids,
and loss wirsels –

see, I'd raither
whummel a single oor
intae the blae o thae wee flo'ers
than live fur a' eternity
in some cauld hivvin.

Wheest, nou, till I spier o ye
will ye haud wi me?

Alan Jenkins

Effects

I held her hand, that was always scarred
From chopping, slicing, from the knives that lay in wait
In bowls of washing-up, that was raw,
The knuckles reddened, rough from scrubbing hard
At saucepan, frying pan, cup and plate
And giving love the only way she knew,
In each cheap cut of meat, in roast and stew,
Old-fashioned food she cooked and we ate;
And I saw that they had taken off her rings,
The rings she'd kept once in her dressing-table drawer
With faded snapshots, long-forgotten things
(Scent-sprays, tortoise-shell combs, a snap or two
From the time we took a holiday 'abroad')
But lately had never been without, as if
She wanted everyone to know she was his wife
Only now that he was dead. And her watch? –
Classic ladies' model, gold strap – it was gone,
And I'd never known her not have *that* on,
Not in all the years they sat together
Watching soaps and game shows I'd disdain
And not when my turn came to cook for her,
Chops or chicken portions, English, bland,
Familiar flavours she said she preferred
To whatever 'funny foreign stuff'
Young people seemed to eat these days, she'd heard;
Not all the weeks I didn't come, when she sat
Night after night and stared unseeing at
The television, at her inner weather,
Heaved herself upright, blinked and poured
Drink after drink, and gulped and stared – the scotch
That, when he was alive, she wouldn't touch,
That was her way to be with him again;
Not later in the psychiatric ward,

Where she blinked unseeing at the wall, the nurses
(Who would steal anything, she said), and dreamt
Of when she was a girl, of the time before
I was born, or grew up and learned contempt,
While the TV in the corner blared
To drown some 'poor soul's' moans and curses,
And she took her pills and blinked and stared
As the others shuffled round, and drooled, and swore...
But now she lay here, a thick rubber band
With her name on it in smudged black ink was all she wore
On the hand I held, a blotched and crinkled hand
Whose fingers couldn't clasp mine any more
Or falteringly wave, or fumble at my sleeve –
The last words she had said were *Please don't leave*
But of course I left; now I was back, though she
Could not know that, or turn her face to see
A nurse bring the little bag of her effects to me.

Emma Jones

Here it is again, spring, 'the renewal'.
People have written about this before.
And the people who track the four seasons,
the hunters who know the weather has changed.

Still, rains happen; there are slow roots that make
progress; something has a hand in the earth
and turns it. Clouds unknot the wind. Bulbs blow.
Their threadbare minds gust outward, turn yellow

eyes to heaven. It answers with the sun.
And the sun is a bulb, a mutual bomb.
The daffodils crack. 'Oh heavens!' they fret,

'Where's your terminus?' The flowers are wan
travellers. They unpack their cases. All
they know, they are. Renewal, rest. Renewal.

Jackie Kay

How they strut about, people in love,
how tall they grow, pleased with themselves,
their hair, glossy, their skin shining.
They don't remember who they have been.

How filmic they are just for this time.
How important they've become – secret, above
the order of things, the dreary mundane.
Every church bell ringing, a fresh sign.

How dull the lot that are not in love.
Their clothes shabby, their skin lustreless;
how clueless they are, hair a mess; how they trudge
up and down streets in the rain,

remembering one kiss in a dark alley,
a touch in a changing-room, if lucky, a lovely wait
for the phone to ring, maybe, baby.
The past with its rush of velvet, its secret hush

already miles away, dimming now, in the late day.

Judy Kendall

WA, HARMONY

The bell goes and I dismiss my class.
Tired and dishevelled, I start to pack away
my papers, wipe off chalk dust,
pack up the tape-deck when, *Teacher, sensei,*

a student hovers, polite, gentle, in need,
at an unobtrusive distance, offering me
a tremulous virgin face while he proceeds
in my hard language to mouth his soft apology

for missing last week's session
because he was unfortunately obliged
(oh teacher, hear out my confession)
to attend the funeral of his grandfather.

His English, slow and careful, broken,
he places in pieces on my gathered notes,
equidistant, partly as if in token
of his loss, partly in the hope

that I will read the spaces in between
the words of me and him, his duty
to the class, his unannounced departure, and fill in
the sadnesses to make consoling harmony,

but, sensing my tiredness and my need to get away
from school at this the end of a long day
and feeling shy, he leaves, and leaves me asking why
in my land we don't make young men this way.

in rain so heavy
with falling blossom, wishing
for you

John Kinsella

The Hierarchy of Sheep – A Report From My Brother

1 *Rams*

To be lamb meat or castrated to wethers
or reign in longevity and fertility
and throw the shearer who can't afford
to hit back, golden balls hanging like trophies,
deep wrinkles genetically engineered
bringing the long merino wool as fine
as the buyer could want, as lambs
of an old ram with a kick so hard
that it takes a couple of roustabouts
to hold it down, will be as boisterous
and determined to take the world on –
'there is a lot of genetics in sheep,
even their temperament'.

A ram horns its way into the blue singlet
of a shearer and through to his belly,
coiled like the spiral matrix of hatred
recognising captivity – fly strike
thickening wool with goo and maggots,
possibly a rogue that's broken down fences,
furious amongst the ewes, savage to its fellows,
headbutting and cracking the competition –
the shearer wastes his enemy with a jet
of aero-start up the nostrils, abusing the farmer
for feeding the bastard lupins and lime
while he watches on nervously, fearing a vengeful shearer
as the feelers sense their way out of the sheath
of the ram's penis – cut by the handpiece
the ram is rendered 'useless',
unable to find the ewe's cunt.

2 *Ewes*

All cut by a shearer at one time or another –
sewn together with dental floss or wearing their scars
gracefully beneath the new season's haute-couture,
role play as if gender has meaning out there –
collectively warding a fox from the lambs.
Earlier the farmer assisted a birth
and then shot a mother polluted by stillbirth –
utilitarian in the way of things. Months back
he'd joked as rams were unleashed
into a ripe flock; up with the crack of dawn,
watching the weather, noticing the comings
and goings of birds. Now rain threatens
and older ewes kick like hell,
all of them full with young, milk veins
up and pumping hard to udders –
somewhere a nick with a blade has a vein
knotted off with needle and thread,
the myth declaring that another takes its place.
'Sometimes ewes get nervous and sensing
their humility is not hard. They get this manic shake
and tears fall from the corners of their eyes.'
A lamb drops in a catching pen.
A shearer aims a teat at his mate
and squirts a shot of milk into his ear.
The shed is full of swearing and laughter.

3 *Wethers*

Low maintenance power houses
scouring the goldfields for scant feed
their wool full of wool spiders, chewing
a shearer's singlet to extract salt
as the handpiece worms off a strip of flesh
and bleats come from somewhere deep
inside, wiry and up against it the farmer
keeping them on a slender thread
to boost the quality of wool – harsh

conditions producing fine strands.
A fly-struck wether with flesh
hanging in sheets and flies erupting
from its ribcage has a fly-killing
poison sprayed into its cavities –
but not even this and the remnants
of testosterone can keep it upright
and a short while later the dull thud
of a gun being fired somewhere outside
moves contrapuntally into the shed,
teasing the buzz of the plant, downtubes whirring,
handpieces snatched in and out of gear.
Even the dead added to the tally.

4 *Lambs*

The assault comes on strong: tailed,
castrated, ringed, earmarked, and mulesed.
Tails gas-axed off. Alive and highly strung
and either moving on to weaner
then hogget then ram, ewe, or wether,
or consumed while the flesh is tender.

Nick Laird

THE LAYERED

doubt

Empty Laird was called that 'cause
his Christian name was Matthew
and his middle one was Thomas.

Towards the end he commented
that by his-self he'd made a sixth
of the disciples, and forgone a life

on the quest for the rest.
And a good book.
Or a decent cause.

fear

Laird Jnr was a tyke, a terrier.

A nit-picker who grew to a hair-splitter,
he was not so much scared of his shadow,
as of its absence. He knew he was see-thru.

It was a very modern kind of terror.

lust

the one   who went on to become   Mrs Laird
the wife   walked into my life
one night   I'd had six or seven pints

and it was either that or fight

she was just the type   I like
chest spilling out of itself   slender-hipped
with a Nubian face closed to the public
waist   my exact hand-span

poised and filmic   she was drinking my usual
unthinkable and very
very do-able   I am not a good man
into my grave into my grave into my grave she was laid

Michael Laskey

Mum put her knitting down and Dad
leant forward in the big armchair
and actually cheered, the news
we were watching, in black and white:
a barrier it had taken an Englishman
to break through. And teamwork too. Brasher
set the pace for the first two laps,
Chataway replaced him and led till the bell
when Bannister went past and, somehow,
powered by the roar, accelerated,
fifty yards clear at the tape.
3 minutes 59.4 seconds.
I re-ran his day again and again:
the dispiriting rain and high winds first thing,
yet how undeterred he did his ward round
and sharpened his spikes, applied graphite
to stop the grit from the cinders sticking
and slowing him down, even so slightly;
how his legs buckled under him afterwards
as he blacked out, and they hauled him up,
hooked his arms round their necks and held him
for the camera, the pain on his face
speaking to me from by far the neatest
page in my scrapbook. Less eloquent was Dad
pinned in the doorway by Budapest,
men throwing stones at the Russian tanks,
their appeal to the west repeatedly broadcast
in broken English, till transmission stopped.
And as for our troops filing up the gang-plank
coming home from Suez – the grinning asses –
he switched them off.

Gwyneth Lewis

Mother Tongue

'I started to translate in seventy-three
in the schoolyard. For a bit of fun
to begin with – the occasional "fuck"
for the bite of another language's smoke
at the back of my throat, its bitter chemicals.
Soon I was hooked on whole sentences
behind the shed, and lessons in Welsh
seemed very boring. I started on print,
Jeeves & Wooster, Dick Francis, James Bond,
in Welsh covers. That worked for a while
until Mam discovered Jean Plaidy inside
a Welsh concordance one Sunday night.
There were ructions: a language, she screamed,
should be for a lifetime. Too late for me.
Soon I was snorting Simenon
and Flaubert. Had to read much more
for any effect. One night I OD'd
after reading far too much Proust.
I came to, but it scared me. For a while
I went Welsh-only but it was bland
and my taste was changing. Before too long
I was back on translating, found that three
languages weren't enough. The "ch"
in German was easy, Rilke a buzz…
For a language fetishist like me
sex is part of the problem. Umlauts make me sweat,
so I need a multilingual man
but they're rare in West Wales and tend to be
married already. If only I'd kept
myself much purer, with simpler tastes,
the Welsh might be living…

                    Detective, you speak
Russian, I hear, and Japanese.
Could you whisper some softly?
I'm begging you. Please…'

Michael Longley

The Holly Bush

in memory of Dorothy Molloy

Frosty Carrigskeewaun. I am breaking ice
Along the salt marsh's soggy margins
And scaring fieldfares out of the holly bush
And redwings, their consorts, chestnut-brown
Flashing one way, chestnut-red another,
Fragments of the January dawn-light
That Killary focuses on the islands
Before it clears the shoulder of Mweelrea.
Caher Island and Inishturk are frosty too.
In the short-lived spotlight they look like cut-
Outs and radiate apricot from within.
I learn of your death in this weather and
Of your book arriving the day after,
Your first and last slim volume. Dorothy,
You read your poems just once and I was there.
The poets you loved are your consorts now.
Golden plovers – a hundred or more – turn
And give back dawn-light from their undersides.
The edge of the dunes wears a fiery fringe.

Mary MacRae

JURY

I'd noticed her hands before, large and quiet
in her lap as she listened through all the words
for the sound she wanted, the call from her scrap
of daughter, fed on demand
while we waited

and I thought of how she'd hold that feather-weight
in one hand while the other cupped the warm head
with its beating fontanelle close to her breast
as if that soft suck and tug
were all the world

and she could forget the knife, (one of a set),
with the serrated edge we'd seen already,
an ordinary kitchen knife, its ten-inch blade
nestling securely inside
a cling-wrapped box.

But it was the photo made me cry – her hand,
in colour, the palm flat for the camera,
fingers stretched apart to show the base of each
cut to the bone, ragged wounds
only half healed:

how painful it must have been to open out
the sheltering fist, uncurl her fingers and feel
the tight scabs crack, exposed for an indifferent
photographer to record
the naked truth.

And the moment all the others led up to
and away from – the moment before her hand
lost its grip on a handle made slippery with
his blood, slid down the blade? – that,
we couldn't see.

Derek Mahon

ROMANCE

after Rimbaud

I

Nothing is serious when you're seventeen.
One evening, sick of the beer and the lemonade,
the noise and bright lights of the café scene,
you sit out under trees on the promenade.

A scent of lime there in the hot June nights.
The air engulfs you with its summery glow;
not far away the wine fumes and the shouts
float up on a soft breeze from down below.

2

You try to fix your gaze on a patch of blue
framed like a picture in the branchy night
pierced by a star, sharp but dissolving now,
quivering slightly, tiny, perfectly white.

A June night! Seventeen! You're getting drunk.
You sip champagne, the stuff goes to your head;
you wander off, imagining some punk
groupie clinging to you or in your bed.

3

The daft heart drifts to popular romance –
when, suddenly, that nice Charmaine goes by,
delightful in the pale glare of the lamps
under her stuffy father's furious eye.

Since you look interesting, if a little weird,
she throws you an alert and lively glance,
two shoes tickety-boo in the boulevard,
and a soppy song dies on your lips at once.

4

Now you're in love (she giggles at your poem) –
in love, until the holidays are through.
Your pals avoid you, love being 'bad form',
and the next day she grants a rendezvous…!

That evening, back to the rowdy café scene,
ordering up the beer and the lemonade.
Nothing is serious when you're seventeen
and lime trees are in leaf on the promenade.

Lorraine Mariner

Thursday

I'm trying to get to work earlier and make
the short walk from Fenchurch Street Station
to the tube at Tower Hill where a guard
is pulling across the gate and commuters
are being evacuated through the gap
and he says it might be closed for ten minutes
half an hour and I think typical walk back
the way I came and on towards Monument
where it's closed again and this guard says
power failure so I walk towards Bank posting
a birthday card to my sister's boyfriend and at
the entrance to Bank it's the same so I phone
my mum who I know will have the radio on
but she says there's nothing on the travel news
you should get a bus to Victoria so I locate
a bus going to Victoria and follow it
to the bus stop and join the crowd that's formed
to wait for the next one and finally it comes
but it's jammed and I watch with admiration
as people with more balls than I'll ever have
leap on through the exit doors until the driver
gets wise and shuts them so I go and find
another bus stop and settle for a bus to Waterloo
with a seat and tell myself I'm not late yet
I'm getting a different view of the city and then
I hear the man behind say explosion and coming
down the stairs a text arrives from my friend
at work asking if I'm ok and so I phone her
and tell her I'm fine and ask her which is the best
bus to catch to Pimlico and then I try my mum
but now she's engaged and I'm standing opposite
the Shell building where my grandma worked
hoping for a 507 and my mum rings and says

it's bad but all my family members are safe in their offices and I'm not to get on any more buses so I start walking through the sirens aiming for the building where my desk is waiting exactly the way I left it yesterday evening.

Glyn Maxwell

THE SNOW VILLAGE

In the age of pen and paper,
when the page was a snow village,
when days the light was leafing through
descended without message,

the nib that struck from heaven
was the sight of a cottage window
lit by the only certain
sign of a life, a candle,

glimpsed by a stranger walking
at a loss through the snow village.
All that can flow can follow
that sighting, though no image,

no face appear – not even
the hand that draws across it –
though the curtains close the vision,
though the stranger end his visit,

though the snow erase all traces
of his passing through the village,
though his step become unknowable
and the whiteness knowledge.

Roger McGough

The Wrong Beds

Life is a hospital ward, and the beds we are put in
are the ones we don't want to be in.
We'd get better sooner if put over by the window.
Or by the radiator, one could suffer easier there.

At night, the impatient soul dreams of faraway places.
The Aegean: all marble and light. Where, upon a beach
as flat as a map, you could bask in the sun like a lizard.

The Pole: where, bathing in darkness, you could watch
the sparks from Hell reflected in a sky of ice. The soul
could be happier anywhere than where it happens to be.

Anywhere but here. We take our medicine daily,
nod politely, and grumble occasionally.
But it is out of our hands. Always the wrong place.
We didn't make our beds, but we lie in them.

Medbh McGuckian

She Is in the Past, She Has this Grace

My mother looks at her watch,
as if to look back over the curve
of her life, her slackening rhythms:
nobody can know her, how she lost herself
evening after evening in that after,
her hourly feelings, the repetition,
delay and failure of her labour
of mourning. The steps space themselves
out, the steps pass, in the mists
and hesitations of the summer,
and within a space which is doubled,
one of us has passed through the other,
though one must count oneself three,
to figure out which of us
has let herself be traversed.

Nothing advances, we don't move,
we don't address one another.
I haven't opened my mouth
except for one remark,
and what remark was that?
A word which appeases the menace
of time in us, reading as if
I were stripping the words
of their ever-mortal high meaning.

She is in dark light, or an openness
that leads to a darkness,
embedded in the wall
her mono-landscape
stays facing the sea
and the harbour activity,
her sea-conscience being ground up

with the smooth time of the deep,
her mourning silhouetted against
the splendour of the sea
which is now to your left,
as violent as it is distant
from all aggressive powers
or any embassies.

And she actively dreams
in the very long ending of this moment,
she is back in her lapping marshes,
still walking with the infinite
step of a prisoner, that former dimension
in which her gaze spreads itself
as a stroke without regarding you,
making you lower your own gaze.

Who will be there,
at that moment, beside her,
when time becomes sacred,
and her voice becomes an opera,
and the solitude is removed
from her body, as if my hand
had been held in some invisible place?

Patrick McGuinness

A History of Doing Nothing

And who would write it?
                    Its first historians
were bemused: it moved, yes, but imperceptibly;
used Time as action did, took place along
the hours, the days, needing somewhere to unfold
like all the things it wasn't. The instruments
designed to trap it could not keep up;
the mind slid off it like water on an oily cloth.
In photographs it was the shadow that seemed
to leak from motion, so that each moving
thing looked always in the company
of its ghost, its own grey opposite.

In wars, it was inferred from the slack rigging
of the warships, the flotillas nuzzling at their moorings;
Heraclitus knew: into the same nothing
nobody stepped twice. Physics was born
when they found that all things bring
a corresponding nothing into being;
metaphysics when they learned that in
a perfect world each thing done
aspired to the same thing left undone.

Its founding epic still used heroes, battles, temples…
only for the space that lay between them. Events?
No; the gaps that separate events,
the hungerless white dreams between awakenings,
slow afternoons that ran aground on boredom.
Its sacred books, pristine from inattention,
promised a paradise where all the squandered energy,
dissipated talents, missed appointments
with destiny or with friends would fuse
in one infinity of cancellation;
where not to have been born was only second best.

What of the doers of nothing?
To the naked eye
they seemed no different from ourselves, surveyed
the low comedy that was activity from beds
or armchairs, suspended in their dusky lives
as the world turns in the emptiness that holds it steady.
Like us, they folded back into Time's pleats
before going, traceless, where the dead go,
soft-footed in the unresisting dark.

Jamie McKendrick

An Encroachment

Now I can take over your side of the bed
I discover the little space between
the bedside and the wall I'd been
unaware of – where you'd made

an installation like a survival kit:
biros specs nailfiles novels magazines
tubes of mild medicaments and creams
one decorative box with nothing in it.

I lift the nothing out and stare at it.
Never has nothing looked more splendid.
Fearful I've left a smudge and marred it
I quickly put it back and shut the lid.

Allison McVety

BOY ON THE BUS

That school gabardine of mine
with its slip-in, slip-out lining,
quilted for winter use,
invisible brown on a bus of standard-issue.
Box-pleats and woollen tights knock knees
with overalls and Crimplene frocks.
In amongst the chiffon,
a crêpe-de-chine square on a shampoo and set.
One man in cavalry-twill, umbrella
tapping a tune on the soles of his brogues. And you
in army & navy surplus, air force blue,
collar raised and cocked, a knapsack
hanging from your shoulder
with the casual cool of *William Hulme*.
I never learned your name or saw you,
beyond your walk to an empty seat,
was never brave enough to look behind
or smile, but I felt you all the same.
Seventeen stops of feeling you.
Boy on the bus, I don't remember what happened
to my gabardine with its slip-in, slip-out lining,
its detachable hood, but I've seen your coat often
at fêtes, in second-hand shops, and once
in the cloakroom of the Festival Hall.
Each time, I've checked the label for your name,
the pockets for mine.

Hilary Menos

BERNARD MANNING PLAYS TOTNES CIVIC HALL

When Bernard Manning played Totnes Civic Hall
the whole town came along. Some bought tickets;
some came to picket in a constructive and caring way.
Terence sang a protest song. We thanked him for sharing.

The wiccans wore woad. Ash sold poems on parchment.
Sky from Tantric Turkeys burned calming patchouli,
assertively chanting the mantra "battery farming
fucks with your karma, man". Bootiful, said Bernard.

The staff of Dartington College took front row seats
in an act of guerrilla theatre. Post-modern, ironic,
Bernard didn't know and didn't care; to him they were
just punters, paying full fare, and not in wheelchairs.

He opened with a sure-fire joke about a gay agoraphobic
who came out and went straight back in, provoking
most of the punters at once, especially the womyn
from Diptford Dykes for Psycho-social Wellbeing.

His carefully chosen gags about wellies and sheep
went down like a fat lamb in slurry. The Mayor had a fit
at his mother-in-law routine. High on quinoa and ginseng,
even the hippies joined in as the crowd stormed the stage.

Bernard fled. As his Roller sped off up the High Street
and shrank to the size of a lentil, the townsfolk united
in transcendental glee. Someone (it may have been me)
said, "That's five hundred quid well spent".

Robert Minhinnick

The Fox in the National Museum of Wales

He scans the frames but doesn't stop,
this fox who has come to the museum today,
his eye in the renaissance
and his brush in the Baroque.

Between dynasties his footprints
have still to fade, between the Shan and the Yung,
the porcelain atoms shivering at his touch,
ah, lighter than the emperor's breath, drinking rice wine from
   the bowl,
daintier than the eunuch pouring wine.

I came as quickly as I could
but already the fox had left the Industrial Revolution behind,
his eye has swept the age of atoms,
the Taj Mahal within the molecule.

The fox is in the fossils and the folios, I cry.
The fox is in Photography and the Folk Studies Department.
The fox is in the flux of the foyer,
the fox is in the flock,
the fox is in the flock.

Now the fox sniffs at the dodo
and at the door of Celtic orthography.
The grave-goods, the chariots, the gods of darkness,
he has made their acquaintance on previous occasions.

There, beneath the leatherbacked turtle he goes,
the turtle black as an oildrum,
under the skeleton of the whale he skedaddles,
the whalebone silver as bubblewrap.

Through the light of Provence moves the fox, through
the Ordovician era and the Sumerian summer,
greyblue the brush on him, this one who has seen so much,
blood on the bristles of his mouth,
and on his suit of iron filings the air fans like silk.

Through the Cubists and the Surrealists
this fox shimmies surreptitiously,
past the artist who has sawn himself in half
under the formaldehyde sky
goes this fox shiny as a silver
fax in his fox coat,
for at a foxtrot travels this fox
backwards and forwards in the museum.

Under the bells of *Brugmansia*
that lull the Ecuadoran botanists to sleep,
over the grey moss of Iceland
further and further goes this fox,
passing the lambs at the feet of Jesus,
through the tear in Dante's cloak.

How long have I legged it
after his legerdemain, this fox
in the labyrinth, this fox that never hurries
yet passes an age in a footfall, this fox
from the forest of the portrait gallery
to Engineering's cornfield sigh?

I will tell you this.
He is something to follow,
this red fellow.
This fox I foster –
he is the future.

No one else
has seen him yet.
But they are closing
the iron doors.

Deborah Moffatt

Along the Coast

All along the coast the young men lie in lonely rooms
Listening for the welcoming sighs of women lying alone
Behind doors left half-closed along darkened landings
On wet dreary nights in the long hours between the last drink
And the start of another day, a woman's sigh inviting the young men
To roam from room to room, from bed to bed, from lips to breast
To thighs, to the wine-drenched oblivion of passionless sex
That helps to pass the lonely night somewhere along the coast.

All along the coast the young men die a little every day,
Their lives slipping away in the hours spent tending bars
Or grooming greens, time spent waiting, watching, dreaming
Of possibilities that might arise, or rueing the chances missed,
Or listening to tales of other men's successes, tales retold,
Later, as their own, to bored women in lonely rooms
Who know better than to hope for anything more than this,
A night of passion in a dreary room somewhere along the coast.

All along the coast young boys with their fathers' faces
Dream of becoming the men their fathers might have been
As their lonely mothers take other men to their beds
On wet dreary nights in the long hours between the last drink
And the start of another day, while young men growing older
Sleep alone in rented rooms, their youth spent, their time gone,
Every dream abandoned, every penny wasted, every chance
Missed, young lives squandered and lost, all along the coast.

Sinéad Morrissey

GENETICS

My father's in my fingers, but my mother's in my palms.
I lift them up and look at them with pleasure –
I know my parents made me by my hands.

They may have been repelled to separate lands,
to separate hemispheres, may sleep with other lovers,
but in me they touch where fingers link to palms.

With nothing left of their togetherness but friends
who quarry for their image by a river,
at least I know their marriage by my hands.

I shape a chapel where a steeple stands.
And when I turn it over,
my father's by my fingers, my mother's by my palms

demure before a priest reciting psalms.
My body is their marriage register.
I re-enact their wedding with my hands.

So take me with you, take up the skin's demands
for mirroring in bodies of the future.
I'll bequeath my fingers, if you bequeath your palms.
We know our parents make us by our hands.

125

Graham Mort

Big in the music business, our father
once kept thirteen pianos in the house.

People found this hard to believe, so we
pictured it for them: a house never short
of ivory or ebony, our fingers waltzing over
slave-trade arpeggios; a house where we
dined from the lid of a baby Broadwood,
skated to school on the Steinway's
borrowed castors, stood pianos on pianos –
the mini-piano inside the concert grand –
and at night whispered the scary German
consonants which captured sleep.

On winter evenings we lit candles in ornate
brass brackets, softening the rooms with
Edwardian light, with homesick songs of
patriotic loss, even employed a blind piano
tuner who only worked at night, each dawn
stepping over traps of snapped strings where
he'd tempered scales to pour cornflakes
or grill toast, the daylight he couldn't see
twisting down figured walnut legs.

My parents slept or argued or made love
on a Bechstein's broken sound-board, behind
a bedroom door of lacquered panels inlaid
with *fleur de lis*; how much of our childhood
was pianissimo, the timbre of felted hammers
falling, how much spent listening then, we never
say, hearkening for wrong chords to brood,
gather, darken the piano's terrible voice.

Andrew Motion

I discovered these men driving a new pile
into the pier. There was all the paraphernalia
of chains, pulleys, cranes, ropes and, as I said,
a wooden pile, a massive affair, swinging

over the water on a long wire hawser.
Everything else was in the massive style
as well, even the men; very powerful men;
very ruminative and silent men ignoring me.

Speech was not something to interest them,
and if they talked at all it was like this –
'Let go', or 'Hold tight': all monosyllables.
Nevertheless, by paying close attention

to the obscure movements of one working
on a ladder by the water's edge, I could tell
that for all their strength and experience
these men were up against a great difficulty.

I cannot say what. Every one of the monsters
was silent on the subject – baffled I thought
at first, but then I realised indifferent
and tired, so tired of the whole business.

The man nearest to me, still saying nothing
but crossing his strong arms over his chest,
showed me that for all he cared the pile
could go on swinging until the crack of Doom.

I should say I watched them at least an hour
and, to do the men justice, their slow efforts

to overcome the secret problem did continue –
then gradually slackened and finally ceased.

One massive man after another abandoned
his position and leaned on the iron rail
to gaze down like a mystic into the water.
No one spoke; no one said what they saw;

though one fellow did spit, and with round eyes
followed the trajectory of his brown bolus
(he had been chewing tobacco)
on its slow descent into the same depths.

The foreman, and the most original thinker,
smoked a cigarette to relieve the tension.
Afterwards, and with a heavy kind of majesty,
he turned on his heel and walked away.

With this eclipse of interest, the incident
was suddenly closed. First in ones and twos,
then altogether, the men followed. That left
the pile still in mid-air, and me of course.

Daljit Nagra

Look We Have Coming to Dover!

'So various, so beautiful, so new…'
Matthew Arnold, 'Dover Beach'

Stowed in the sea to invade
the alfresco lash of a diesel-breeze
ratcheting speed into the tide, brunt with
gobfuls of surf phlegmed by cushy come-and-go
tourists prow'd on the cruisers, lording the ministered waves.

Seagull and shoal life
vexing their blarnies upon our huddled
camouflage past the vast crumble of scummed
cliffs, scramming on mulch as thunder unbladders
yobbish rain and wind on our escape hutched in a Bedford van.

Seasons or years we reap
inland, unclocked by the national eye
or stabs in the back, teemed for breathing
sweeps of grass through the whistling asthma of parks,
burdened, ennobled – poling sparks across pylon and pylon.

Swarms of us, grafting in
the black within shot of the moon's
spotlight, banking on the miracle of sun –
span its rainbow, passport us to life. Only then
can it be human to hoick ourselves, bare-faced for the clear.

Imagine my love and I,
our sundry others, Blair'd in the cash
of our beeswax'd cars, our crash clothes, free,
we raise our charged glasses over unparasol'd tables
East, babbling our lingoes, flecked by the chalk of Britannia!

Sean O'Brien

Fantasia on a Theme of James Wright

There are miners still
In the underground rivers
Of West Moor and Palmersville.

There are guttering cap-lamps bound up in the roots
Where the coal is beginning again.
They are sinking slowly further

In between the shiftless seams,
To black pools in the bed of the world.
In their long home the miners are labouring still –

Gargling dust, going down in good order,
Their black-braided banners aloft,
Into flooding and firedamp, there to inherit

Once more the tiny corridors of the immense estate
They line with prints of Hedley's *Coming Home*.
We hardly hear of them.

There are the faint reports of spent economies,
Explosions in the ocean floor,
The thud of iron doors sealed once for all

On prayers and lamentation,
On pragmatism and the long noyade
Of a class which dreamed itself

Immortalized by want if nothing else.
The singing of the dead inside the earth
Is like the friction of great stones, or like the rush

Of water into newly opened darkness. My brothers,
The living will never persuade them
That matters are otherwise, history done.

Ciaran O'Driscoll

Please Hold

This is the future, my wife says.
We are already there, and it's the same
as the present. Your future, here, she says.
And I'm talking to a robot on the phone.
The robot is giving me countless options,
none of which answer to my needs.
Wonderful, says the robot
when I give him my telephone number.
And Great, says the robot
when I give him my account number.
I have a wonderful telephone number
and a great account number,
but I can find nothing to meet my needs
on the telephone, and into my account
(which is really the robot's account)
goes money, my money, to pay for nothing.
I'm paying a robot for doing nothing.
This call is free of charge, says the robot.
Yes but I'm paying for it, I shout,
out of my wonderful account
into my great telephone bill.
Wonderful, says the robot.
And my wife says, This is the future.
I'm sorry, I don't understand, says the robot.
Please say Yes or No.
Or you can say Repeat or Menu.
You can say Yes, No, Repeat or Menu,
or you can say Agent if you'd like to talk
to someone real, who is just as robotic.
I scream Agent! and am cut off,
and my wife says, This is the future.
We are already there and it's the same
as the present. Your future, here, she says.

And I'm talking to a robot on the phone,
and he is giving me no options
in the guise of countless alternatives.
We appreciate your patience. Please hold.
Eine Kleine Nachtmusik. Please hold.
Eine Kleine Nachtmusik. Please hold.
Eine fucking Kleine Nachtmusik.
And the robot transfers me to himself.
Your call is important to us, he says.
And my translator says, This means
your call is not important to them.
And my wife says, This is the future.
And my translator says, Please hold
means that, for all your accomplishments,
the only way you can now meet your needs
is by looting. Wonderful, says the robot.

Please hold. Please grow old. Please grow cold.
Please do what you're told. Grow old. Grow cold.
This is the future. Please hold.

Dennis O'Driscoll

OUT OF CONTROL

Worry on, mothers: you have
good reason to lose sleep,
to let imaginations run riot
as you lie in bed, not counting sheep
but seeing sons and daughters
like lambs led to slaughter
in the road kill of Friday nights.

Remain on standby, mothers –
you never know your luck –
for the knock that would break
the silence like the shock
of a metallic impact against brick.
Keep imagining a police beacon,
a blue moon shattering the darkness.

Lie warily, mothers, where,
eighteen years before, conception
took place in the black of night,
a secret plot; wait restlessly,
as if for a doctor's test,
to find out whether
you are still with child.

Caitríona O'Reilly

AUTOBIOGRAPHY

Here the weather has its own spectrum,
a seemingly limitless palette. To the north
a chain of swollen, dark green mountains.
Mostly they are smooth and stippled with heather,
then too I've seen them snow-capped, gleaming.
The run of mountains ends with the seaward
drop of Bray Head's ponderous mossy forehead.
Between there and here are miles of salty fields.
Clattering by on the littoral track after a flood
I've seen the miserable cattle islanded
on the high ground of their uneven fields.
In summer those meadows burn with gorse.
An intermittent shot to scare the birds
is all that disturbs the gelatinous air –
that, and the odd vertical string of bonfire smoke.
The distant hill on which my town is built quivers.
I live between three Victorian piers on the bay's industrial side.
The bay smiles, it is full of flattened shiny water
sucking quietly at the shore and piers. All night
I adjust my own breath to its eternally regular breaking.
Less frequently now, a cargo ship sets up
a prehistoric rumble in the waters of the bay
and docks, raising its hatches with a metal groan.
Two synchronised forklift trucks neatly stack
the planks of timber, balletic and mechanical.
When the ships brought raw cement, plumes of dust
would sweep across the bay, coating our windows and doors.
On the east side of my house is an ancient castle keep
of blackest rock, that leans like a fin
from the back of the sea. I live in the shadow
of the shadow of a castle's walls.
They have fallen to hummocks of bright grass
that we played in as children,

wriggling into nests and hidey-holes.
The dark beach in the lee of the castle
is where Saint Patrick put ashore. He soon left,
shocked at the natives' epic unfriendliness:
They knocked Saint Manntan's front teeth down his neck.
Among the shells and shingle of the beach
are opalescent nuggets of glass, rounded and stone-smooth
from aeons rolling on the ocean floor.
Was it really from wrecked galleons they came?
But still there is the bay's omega, its theatre of weather,
a glass bowl for the sky to play in. The sea has no colour
save what weather brings. I've watched the sky and sea
go up in flames at dusk, though mostly they're an angry grey.
Now any horizon of mine must be nine-tenths sky.

Helen Oswald

THE PASSION

That year it made a change from cowboys and indians,
my brother's hyena yelp as he scalped me again.
Comanche. We knew about the thrill of blood.

Out in the greenhouse, we sawed wooden stakes
recast from former roles piercing the hearts
of vampires, to nail three crosses.

I tore old bed sheets into strips of loincloth,
anointed the feet of a bear with Pears shampoo
and left it overnight in a geranium Gethsemane.

Our reluctant parents watched
at an upstairs window, mortified and yet
unable to wash their hands of it.

Beneath the holly tree that had supplied
a crown of thorns, two gollies, thieves,
awaited Christ, and me and my brother

stretched to an unruly crowd, yelling:
"Crucify him! Crucify him!"
Two small gods making it all happen.

Marita Over

SPIDERS

A Rorschach inkblot is
fastened on the porcelain.
Will not respond at first, nor wash away.
Does not thin. Does not appear

to bloom into a colour chart
like those ink chromatograms
whose wet throats bleed the secrets of their
blackest composition.

It is an alert black hand
around my heart, squeezing it dry.
This is a stain that stays.
No lady can easily wash it away.

Yet all through October
the creature thrived on our lavender.
Females fattened
gently in their spinnings.

Soft flesh, speckled
like mute thrushes,
or sun-warmed miniature toads
intent on digestion.

And our garden all autumn
like a good sleep you wake from
the threads to your hinterland cut and forgotten,
contained them out of sight and mind.

November now though, with both taps on,
the gushing lifts her too light body
on a swirl that spins her
drifting towards the plug-hole.

There she staggers, little hag,
on a penny-pinching stint,
making thrifty
silk of the water.

Ruth Padel

Shall I tell how she went to India
At the age of eighty
For a week in the monsoon

    Because her last unmarried son
    Was getting married to a girl
    With a mask of yellow turmeric on her face

At the shrine of Maa Markoma
In the forest where Orissa's last
Recorded human sacrifice took place?

    How this mother of mine rode a motorbike,
    Pillion, up a leopard-and-leeches path
    Through jungle at full moon,

Getting off to shove away
The sleeping buffalo,
Puddled shaves of sacred calf?

    How she who hates all frills
    Watched her feet painted scarlet henna,
    Flip-flop pattern between the toes

And backward swastikas at heel, without a murmur?
How she climbed barefoot to Shiva
Up a rock-slide – where God sat

    Cross-legged, navy blue,
    On a boulder above his cave,
    One hand forbidding anyone impure,

Or wearing leather, to come in?
How she forded Cobra River
In a hundred degrees at noon

To reach the God's familiar – his little bull of stone,
A pinky blaze of ribbons, bells, hibiscus –
And, lifelong sceptic that she is,

The eyes of all the valley on her – Tribal, Hindu,
Atheist and Christian – bowed? Shall I tell how you
Laughed fondly at me for my pride

In her? How I wait on the miracle
Of your breath in my ear? Shall I tell
Them? Yes. Tell that.

Don Paterson

O Natalie, O TBA, O Tusja: I had long assumed the
terrorist's balaclava that you sport on the cover of *Annulé* –
    which was, for too long, the only image of you I
possessed – was there to conceal some ugliness or deformity
    or perhaps merely spoke (and here, I hoped against
hope) of a young woman struggling
    with a crippling shyness. How richly this latter theory
has been confirmed by my Googling!

O who is this dark angel with her unruly Slavic eyebrows
ranged like two duelling pistols, lightly sweating in the pale
light of the TTF screen?
    O behold her shaded, infolded concentration, her
heartbreakingly beautiful face so clearly betraying the true
focus of one not merely content – as, no doubt, were others
at the Manöver Elektronische Festival in Wien –
    to hit *play* while making some fraudulent correction to a
volume slider
    but instead deep in the manipulation of some complex
real-time software, such as Ableton Live, MAX/MSP or
Supercollider.

O Natalie, how can I pay tribute to your infinitely
versatile blend of Nancarrow, Mille Plateaux, Venetian
Snares, Xenakis, Boards of Canada and Nobukazu Takemura
    to say nothing of those radiant pads – so strongly
reminiscent of the mid-century bitonal pastoral of Charles
Koechlin in their harmonic bravura –
    or your fine vocals, which, while admittedly limited in
range and force, are nonetheless so much more affecting
    than the affected Arctic whisperings of those
interchangeably dreary
    Stinas and Hannes and Björks, being in fact far closer in
spirit to a kind of glitch-hop Blossom Dearie?

I have also deduced from your staggeringly ingenious
employment of some pretty basic wavetables
     that unlike many of your East European counterparts, all
your VST plug-ins, while not perhaps the best available
     probably all have a legitimate upgrade path – indeed I
imagine your entire DAW as pure as the driven snow, and not
in any way buggy or virusy
     which makes me love you more, demonstrating as it does
an excess of virtue given your country's well-known talent for
software piracy.

     Though I should confess that at times I find your habit of
maxxing
     the range with those bat-scaring ring-modulated
sine-bursts and the more distressing psychoacoustic properties
of phase inversion in the sub-bass frequencies somewhat taxing
     you are nonetheless as beautiful as the mighty Boards
themselves in your shameless organicising of the code,
     as if you had mined those saws and squares and ramps
straight from the Georgian motherlode.

     O Natalie – I forgive you everything, even your
catastrophic adaptation of those lines from 'Dylan's' already
shite
     Do Not Go Gentle Into That Good Night
     in the otherwise magnificent 'Sleepwalkers', and when
you open up those low-
     pass filters in what sounds like a Minimoog emulation
they seem to open in my heart also.

     O Natalie: know that I do not, repeat, do *not* imagine
you with a reconditioned laptop bought with a small grant
from the local arts cooperative in the cramped back bedroom
of an ex-communist apartment block in Tbilisi or Kutaisi
     but at the time of writing your biographical details are
extremely hazy;
     however, I feel sure that by the time this poem sees the
light of day Wire magazine will have honoured you with a

far more extensive profile than you last merited when
mention of that wonderful Pharrell remix

was sandwiched between longer pieces on the notorious
Kyoto-based noise guitarist Idiot O'Clock, and a woman
called Sonic Pleasure who plays the housebricks.

However this little I have gleaned: firstly, that you are
married to Thomas Brinkmann, whose records are boring –
an opinion I held long before love carried me away –

and secondly, that TBA

is not an acronym, as I had first assumed, but Georgian
for 'lake' – in which case it probably has a silent 't', like
'Tbilisi', and so is pronounced *baa*

which serendipitously rhymes a bit with my only other
word of Georgian, being your term for 'mother' which is
'dada', or possibly 'father' which is 'mama'.

I doubt we will ever meet, unless this somehow reaches
you on the wind;

we will never sit with a glass of tea in your local
wood-lined café while I close-question you on how you
programmed that unbelievably great snare on 'Wind',

of such brickwalled yet elastic snap it sounded exactly
like a 12" plastic ruler bent back and released with great
violence on the soft gong

of a large white arse, if not one white for long.

But Natalie – Tusja, if I may – I will not pretend I hold
much hope for us, although I have, I confess, worked up my
little apologia:

I am not like those other middle-agey I-
DM enthusiasts: I have none of their hangdog pathos,
my geekery is the dirty secret that it should be

and what I lack in hair, muscle-tone and rugged good
looks I make up for with a dry and ready wit... but I know
that time and space conspire against me.

At least, my dear, let me wish you the specific best:
may you be blessed
with the wonderful instrument you deserve, fitted –
at the time of writing – with a 2 Ghz dual-core Intel chip
and enough double-pumped DDR2 RAM for the most
CPU-intensive processes;
        then no longer will all those gorgeous acoustic spaces
    be accessible only via an offline procedure involving a
freeware convolution reverb and an imperfectly recorded
impulse response of the Concertgebouw made illegally with a
hastily-erected stereo pair and an exploded crisp bag
        for I would have all your plug-ins run in real-time, in the
blameless zero-latency heaven of the 32-bit floating-point
environment, with no buffer-glitch or freeze or dropout or lag;
        I would also grant you a golden midi controller, of such
responsiveness, smoothness of automation, travel and increment
        that you would think it a transparent intercessor, a mere
copula, and feel machine and animal suddenly blent.

        This I wish you as I leave Inverkeithing and Fife
        listening to *Trepa N* for the two hundred and thirty-fourth
time in my life
        with every hair on my right arm rising in non-fascistic
one-armed salutation
        towards Natalie, Tba, my Tusja, and all the mountain
lakes of her small nation.

Clare Pollard

> *'And let the lesson to be – to be yersel's,*
> *Ye needna fash gin it's to be ocht else.*
> *To be yersel's – and to mak' that worth bein'…'*
>   Hugh MacDiarmid,
>   'A Drunk Man Looks at a Thistle'

> *' Let me take you on a journey to a foreign land…'*
>   William Hague

I

Dusk-light; the news tells of another train derailed,
and shoppers buying up the shops, and livestock
being herded to the chop – their chops unfit to eat –
and politicians once more putting foot to mouth.
Through my east-end window –

                              over the tangled tree,
the council houses: some sardined with children,
catering-sized gallon tubs of cooking oil empty beside their bins;
some sheltering one of the three million children still in poverty;
some sold to Thatcher's fortunate –
now worth hundreds of thousands, more,
with rents devised to make even the well-off poor –
over the kids and dogs on a hanky of grass,
the burnt-out car, the hush-hush trendy warehouse bar,
ISLAM UNITE scrawled on a wall –

a man's voice trails its skittering wail across the sky,
and all around me people are preparing to pray
to a God to whom I am one of the damned.

II

And what did our great-grandmothers taste?
Perhaps pie and mash and jellied eels, or hash, pease pudding,
cobbler, cottage pie,
                                    pasties and pickled eggs.
When I was small there was still Spam and jellied ham –
semolina, parkin, treacle tart.
Why have we not stood with our mothers,
floured and flushed beside the oven door,
watching our first Yorkshire puddings:
how their globed bellies swell?
Why was this not passed daughter to daughter?
When did the passing stop?
When did we choose to steal instead
from the daughters of all those we have hated or hurt:
gnocchi, noodles, couscous, naan, falafel, jerk?
For dinner I have chicken dupiaza from a foil tray –
how fitting England's national dish is not homemade but takeaway.
Through thrift – the rent is due – I boil my own rice up,
long-grain American.

III

You're so fortunate, they would exclaim, as I took photographs
of them beside King's Chapel, or of willows washing
their hair in the Cam, *to have all of this history around you.*

England's history is medieval pogroms;
it is Elizabeth, her skin a crust of Dover-white,
loosing galleons to pillage fruits, tobacco, men.
The bulging-eyed thieves swinging to the crowd's delight
metres from Shakespeare's Globe;
                                    stripping the churches;
Becket bleeding buckets on the floor;
and work-houses for the poor,
and the slave-trade; and raping the wife –

lie back and think of… crinolines, Crimea.
Missionaries hacking their one true path through the jungle.
Winston swearing: *We will fight them on the beaches!*

These people held the cargo of my genes within their blood.
Not all were good.
                         But how can I be held up as accountable?
And yet, all of the good they earned, and blessed me with
brings with it blame. Today I filled a form in –
ticked *White British* with a cringe of shame.

I am educated, middle-class, housed, well.
I am fat and rich on history's hell.

IV

I remember bracken, and heather, and a gusty, gutsy
wind, and a plastic tub of windberries that filled
and emptied, its ink writing a whodunit on my face.

I remember Southport, where granny said fine ladies had once
gone to purchase linens, and the best. Catching the miniature
train down to Happy-Land, and my name in wet sand,

and my grandfather towelling the sand off my legs,
and then our picnic in the car – tinned salmon sandwiches,
a flask of tea, crosswords. A Penguin biscuit.

I remember sitting in an American bar having to squint
to read about abortion laws by the dim candlelight,
and sipping my six-dollar Cosmopolitan – with a dollar tip –

and thinking of our local; its open fire, the rain
on its windows, and you in it. Maybe on a Sunday
after a walk on the heath, and lamb with mint sauce,

and thinking how I never could leave.

V

Just finishing off the curry, when the football starts.
An England game. Satellites are readying themselves
to bounce the match around the globe,
and prove that we are not the power we were.

The crowd belts out 'God Save the Queen',
though they do not believe in God or Queen;
their strips red, white and blue –
two of these being borrowed hues; loaned colours we use
to drown out the white noise of ourselves.
We are the whitest of the white:
                              once this meant *right* –
Christ's holy light; the opposite of night, or black –
but now it only points to lack, the blank of who we are.

Who ever celebrates St George's Day?
And did you hear the one about the Englishman…?

A friend of mine at home's a Bolton Wanderers fan:
they chant *White Army*.

VI

And then the news again, at ten –
sometimes it makes you want to pack and leave it all:

the floods, the fuel, the teacher shortage in the schools,
the bombing of Iraq, the heart attacks, long working hours
and little sex, racist police, cigarette tax, grants all axed,
three million children still in poverty,
the burnt out car, the takeaway,
the headlines about Krauts, the lager louts,
the wobbly bridge they built, the colonial guilt,
the needless pain, the rain, the rain,

the pogroms, the pink globe, the tangled tree,
the Raj, the rape, the linens,
all the endless fucking cups of tea...

but everyone speaks English now,

and sometimes, a voice trails its skittering wail across the sky,
and I feel not just gratitude, but pride.

Jacob Polley

The Cheapjack

What do I have for as near as damn it?
What do I sell but I'm giving away?
   Might I pick my own pockets
   and slit my own throat
and dump myself dead in a shop doorway?

Daffodils, bird whistles, bobble hats,
fickle fish, Slinkies, your name spelled in wire;
   caterpillars, mouse mats,
   trick plastic dog-shit,
conniptions, predictions and God's own fire.

I've bargained myself to Bedlam and back,
and a wonder it is that I'm not less flesh,
   for I'd sell you the scraps,
   the loose skin, the slack,
the tips of my toes and the last of my breath

and might as well for the good my breath's done;
I've blown suits, jobs, marriages, houses and lands:
   I'm a man overcome
   by his profligate tongue,
and if you get close, you can stand where I stand.

What'll it cost? Not as much as you think.
What have you got? That'll do. Here's my nod,
   here's my wink,
   here's my blood for the ink.
I'm begging you now: my life for the lot.

Andrea Porter

JOHN F. KENNEDY *d.*1963

I was sitting crosslegged in my grey school skirt
in front of Josie Hibbert's tiny Bakelite TV.
Upstairs her Mum was dying of something quiet.
We ran upstairs to tell her and she cried.

MARTIN LUTHER KING *d.*1968

I was with a black haired boy called Dave,
in his room still decorated with Noddy wallpaper.
Downstairs his Mum cooked egg and chips
in a long sleeved blouse to hide the bruises.

STEPHEN BANTU BIKO *d.*1977

I was walking through the Arndale Centre.
A TV called to me from a shop window.
Two stores up a shabby man was shouting.
Security was there telling him to move on.

JOHN LENNON *d.*1980

I was sitting at a green Formica table.
Across from me a girl was smoking roll ups.
She'd gouged zigzags into both her arms.
We drank tea as she picked at the scabs.

Peter Porter

LAST WORDS

In the beginning was the Word,
Not just the word of God but sounds
Where Truth was clarified or blurred.
Then Rhyme and Rhythm did the rounds
And justified their jumps and joins
By glueing up our lips and loins.

Once words had freshness on their breath.
The Poet who saw first that Death
Has only one true rhyme was made
The Leader of the Boys' Brigade.
Dead languages can scan and rhyme
Like birthday cards and *Lilac Time*.

And you can carve words on a slab
Or tow them through the air by plane,
Tattoo them with a painful jab
Or hang them in a window pane.
Unlike our bodies which decay,
Words, first and last, have come to stay.

Richard Price

from A Spelthorne Bird List

Coot

The coot was a pint of stout. It slipped out from The Ferry
during a fight. Mathematically white, it was plunged by its beak
in mathematical black. To uppity swans it does not signify. The
same goes for Joe Duck.

Heron

A greying Senior Lecturer in Fish Studies (Thames Valley), he
stands in frozen hop concentration, regarding a lectern only he
can see. Still, he gets results. He's hoping for a chair.

Kingfisher

Blue. I mean green. Blue, green.   Gone.

Sheenagh Pugh

NIGHT NURSES IN THE MORNING

No bench in the bus shelter; they slump
against caving perspex, dragging the Silk Cut

deep into their lungs, eyes closed, holding
the moment, then letting a long breath go.

And they don't talk. Swollen ankles above
big white boat-shoes, dreams of foot-spas.

Pale pink pale green pale blue, even without
the washed-out uniforms you could tell them

from us other early-morning faces
going in, starting the day. We eye them sideways

as they fall into seats, ease their shoes off.
More pallid than colliers or snooker players,

the vampires of mercy. All their haunts lie near
this bus route: here's St Stephen's Hospice,

where folk go to die, there, the Lennox Home
for Elderly Ladies. Just round the bend,

the other granny-park, where I walked past
an open window one evening when the lilac

was out, and heard a young voice scream, over and over,
You bitch, you bitch, and another tone,

querulous and high, a complaining descant
to her theme. They both sounded desperate.

People who live by night aren't quite canny.
We let them keep things running, avoid their eyes,

resenting the way they don't seem to need us there.
What do you do, in the corners of darkness

where we sweep the inconvenient? What is it
you never say to each other on the bus?

As our faces wake, exhaustion silvers
the back of their eyes: not windows but mirrors.

Sally Read

INSTRUCTION

Check: water, soap, a folded sheet, a shroud.
Close cubicle curtains; light's swallowed
in hospital green. Our man lies dense
with gravity: an arm, his head, at angles
as if dropped from a great height. There is
a fogged mermaid from shoulder to wrist,
nicotine-stained teeth, nails dug with dirt –
a labourer then, one for the women.
A smooth drain to ivory is overtaking
from the feet. Wash him, swiftly, praising
in murmurs like your mother used,
undressing you when asleep. Dry carefully.
If he complained at the damp when alive, dry
again. Remove teeth, all tags, rip off elastoplast –
careful now, each cell is snuffing its lights,
but black blood still spurts. Now,
the shroud (opaque, choirboy ruff), fasten
it on him, comb his hair to the right. Now
he could be anyone. Now wrap in the sheet,
like a parcel, start at his feet. Swaddle (not
tight nor too loose) – it's an art, sheafing
this bundle of untied, heavy sticks. Hesitate
before covering his face, bandaging warm
wet recesses of eyes, mouth. Your hands
will prick – an animal sniffing last traces
of life. Cradle the head, bind it with tape
and when it lolls, lovingly against your chest,
lower it gently as a bowl brimmed with water.
Collect tags, teeth, washbowl. Open
the window, let the soul fly. Through
green curtains the day will tear: cabs, sun-
glare, rain. Remember to check:
tidied bed, emptied cabinet, sheeted form –

observe him recede to the flux between seconds,
the slowness of sand. Don't loiter. Slide
back into the ward's slipstream; pick up
your pace immediately.

◆

Robin Robertson

La Stanza Delle Mosche

The room sizzles in the morning sun;
a tinnitus of flies at the bright windows,
butting and dunting the glass. One dings
off the light, to the floor, vibrating blackly,
pittering against the wall before taxi
and take-off – another low moaning flight,
another fruitless stab at the world outside.
They drop on my desk, my hands,
and spin their long deaths on their backs
on the white tiles, first one way
then the other, tiny humming tops that
stop and start: a sputter of bad wiring,
whining to be stubbed out.

Fiona Sampson

From the Adulteress's Songbook

Because he could not live with me
    because he was my life,
the truth that could not come to be
    because I was a wife,

he emptied meaning from the words
    that should have guided me –
I kept the compass, lost the lode
    of how things ought to be

and wandered out among the forms
    that might inform a life,
finding cold comfort in each warmth
    because I was a wife.

Myra Schneider

GOULASH

for Grevel

A crucial ingredient is the right frame of mind
so abandon all ideas of getting on. Stop pedalling,
dismount, go indoors and give yourself masses of time.
Then begin by heating a pool of oil in a frying pan
and, Mrs Beeton style, take a dozen onions
even though the space you're working in is smaller
than the scullery in a Victorian mansion. Pull off
the papery wrappings and feel the shiny globes' solidity
before you chop. Fry the segments in three batches.
Don't fuss about weeping eyes, with a wooden spoon
ease the pieces as they turn translucent and gold.
When you've browned but not burnt the cubes of beef
marry meat and onions in a deep pan, bless the mixture
with stock, spoonfuls of paprika, tomato purée
and crushed garlic. Enjoy the Pompeian-red warmth.
Outside, the sun is reddening the pale afternoon
and you'll watch as it sinks behind blurring roofs,
the raised arms of trees, the intrepid viaduct.
In the kitchen's triumph of colour and light the meat
is softening and everything in the pot is seeping
into everything else. By now you're thinking of love:
the merging which bodies long for, the merging
that's more than body. While you're stirring the stew
it dawns on you how much you need darkness.
It lives in the underskirts of thickets where sealed buds
coddle green, where butterflies folded in hibernation,
could be crumpled leaves. It lives in the sky that carries
a deep sense of blue and a thin boat of moon angled
as if it's rocking. It lives in the silent larder and upstairs
in the airing cupboard where a padded heart pumps
heat, in the well of bed where humans lace together.

Time to savour all this as the simmering continues,
as you lay the table and place at its centre a small jug
in which you've put three tentative roses and sprigs
of rosemary. At last you will sit down with friends
and ladle the dark red goulash onto plates bearing
beds of snow-white rice. As you eat the talk will be bright
as the garnets round your neck, as those buried
with an Anglo-Saxon king in a ship at Sutton Hoo,
and the ring of words will carry far into the night.

Jo Shapcott

Of Mutability

Too many of the best cells in my body
are itching, feeling jagged, turning raw
in this spring chill. It's two thousand and four
and I don't know a soul who doesn't feel small
among the numbers. Razor small.
Look down these days to see your feet
mistrust the pavement and your blood tests
turn the doctor's expression grave.

Look up to catch eclipses, gold leaf, comets,
angels, chandeliers, out of the corner of your eye,
join them if you like, learn astrophysics, or
learn folksong, human sacrifice, mortality,
flying, fishing, sex without touching much.
Don't trouble, though, to head anywhere but the sky.

Kathryn Simmonds

The Boys in the Fish Shop

This one winds a string of plastic parsley
around the rainbow trout,
punnets of squat lobster and marinated anchovy,
the dish of jellied eels
in which a spoon stands erect.
He's young, eighteen perhaps,
with acne like the mottled skin of some pink fish,
and there's gold in his ear, the hoop of a lure.
The others aren't much older,
bantering in the back room,
that den of stinking mysteries
where boxes are carried.

The fish lie around all day,
washed-up movie stars
stunned on their beds of crushed ice.
The boys take turns to stare
through the wide glass window,
hands on hips, an elbow on a broom,
lost for a moment in warm waters until
Yes darling, what can I get you?
and their knives return to the task,
scraping scales in a sequin shower,
splitting parcels of scarlet and manganese.
Their fingers know a pound by guesswork,
how to unpeel smoked salmon,
lay it fine as lace on cellophane.
A girl walks past, hair streaming,
and the boy looks up,
still gripping his knife, lips parting in a slack O.

Catherine Smith

THE NEW BRIDE

Dying, darling, is the easy bit. Fifty paracetamol,
bride-white and sticking in the throat, ten shots
of Johnny Walker, and the deed is done.
A twilight day of drowsing, then the breathing
slows to a whisper, like a sinner in Confession.

Death is dead easy. No, what happens next
is the difficulty. You bastard, howling in public,
snivelling over photos, ringing round for consolation.
And you have me burnt, like a dinner gone wrong,
you keep the charred remains of me on show

at the Wake, inviting everyone I hate. Oh God,
they come in packs, sleek as rats with platitudes
and an eye on my half of the bed, hoping to find
leftover skin, a hint of fetid breath. I leave them
no hairs on the pillow; there are none to leave.

And a year to the day since I shrug off the yoke
of life, you meet the new bride. In group therapy.
You head straight for a weeper and wailer,
telling strangers all her little tragedies. You love
the way she languishes, her tears sliming your neck,

you give into her on vile pink Austrian blinds.
The Wedding is a riot of white nylon. Everybody
drinks your health and hers, the simpering bitch.
She and Delia Smith keep you fat and happy
as a pig in shit. I want her cells to go beserk.

Some nights I slip between you. The new bride
sleeps buttoned up, slug-smug in polyester. You,

my faithless husband, turn over in your dreams,
and I'm there, ice-cold and seeking out your eyes
and for a moment you brush my lips, and freeze.

John Stammers

Ask Them

Ask them all where it is hid;
ask the old man and the kid,
fortune tellers in their stripy tents,
circus artists, governments,
cyclists round the velodromes,
Rosicrucians, garden gnomes.
Enquire politely of city women in their fashion heels;
ask the sturgeons, lampreys and the conger eels.
Go to Lourdes, Delphi, London Zoo;
lobby wolverine and kangaroo.
Humbly petition the Arapaho
(if it were known, surely they would know).
Look in each house, each studio flat;
pray to God from Mt Ararat.
Ask them, ask them every one;
examine the poles, go to the sun.
You will not find a single clue;
it is no longer there for you.

George Szirtes

for Helen Suzman

Nothing happens until something does.
Everything remains just as it was
And all you hear is the distant buzz
Of nothing happening till something does.

A lot of small hands in a monstrous hall
can make the air vibrate
and even shake the wall;
a voice can break a plate
or glass, and one pale feather tip
the balance on a sinking ship.

It's the very same tune that has been sung
time and again by those
whose heavy fate has hung
on the weight that they oppose,
the weight by which are crushed
the broken voices of the hushed.

But give certain people a place to stand
a lever, a fulcrum, a weight,
however small the hand,
the object however great,
it is possible to prove
that even Earth may be made to move.

Nothing happens until something does,
and hands, however small,
fill the air so the buzz
of the broken fills the hall
as levers and fulcrums shift
and the heart like a weight begins to lift.

Nothing happens until something does.
Everything remains just as it was
And all you hear is the distant buzz
Of nothing happening. Then something does.

Adam Thorpe

ON HER BLINDNESS

My mother could not bear being blind,
to be honest. One shouldn't say it.

One should hide the fact that catastrophic
handicaps are hell; one tends to hear,

publicly, from those who bear it
like a Roman, or somehow find joy

in the fight. She turned to me, once,
in a Paris restaurant, still not finding

the food on the plate with her fork,
or not so that it stayed on (try it

in a pitch-black room) and whispered,
'It's living hell, to be honest, Adam.

If I gave up hope of a cure, I'd bump
myself off.' I don't recall what I replied,

but it must have been the usual sop,
inadequate: the locked-in son.

She kept her dignity, though, even when
bumping into walls like a dodgem; her sense

of direction did not improve, when cast
inward. 'No built-in compass,' as my father

joked. Instead, she pretended to ignore
the void, or laughed it off.

Or saw things she couldn't see
and smiled, as when the kids would offer

the latest drawing, or show her their new toy –
so we'd forget, at times, that the long,

slow slide had finished in a vision
as blank as stone. For instance, she'd continued

to drive the old Lanchester
long after it was safe

down the Berkshire lanes. She'd visit exhibitions,
admire films, sink into television

while looking the wrong way.
Her last week alive (a fortnight back)

was golden weather, of course,
the autumn trees around the hospital

ablaze with colour, the ground royal
with leaf-fall. I told her this, forgetting,

as she sat too weak to move, staring
at nothing. 'Oh yes, I know,' she said,

'it's lovely out there.' Dying has made her
no more sightless, but now she can't

pretend. Her eyelids were closed
in the coffin; it was up to us to believe

she was watching, somewhere, in the end.

Tim Turnbull

ODE ON A GRAYSON PERRY URN

Hello! What's all this here? A kitschy vase
  some Shirley Temple manqué has knocked out
delineating tales of kids in cars
  on crap estates, the Burberry clad louts
who flail their motors through the smoky night
  from Manchester to Motherwell or Slough,
    creating bedlam on the Queen's highway.
Your gaudy evocation can, somehow,
  conjure the scene, without inducing fright
    as would a *Daily Express* exposé,

can bring to mind the throaty turbo roar
  of hatchbacks tuned almost to breaking point,
the joyful throb of UK garage or
  of house imported from the continent
and yet educe a sense of peace, of calm –
  the screech of tyres and the nervous squeals
    of girls, too young to quite appreciate
the peril they are in, are heard, but these wheels
  will not lose traction, skid and flip, no harm
    befall these children. They will stay out late

forever, pumped on youth and ecstasy,
  on alloy, bass and arrogance, and speed
the back lanes, the urban gyratory,
  the wide motorways, never having need
to race back home, for work next day, to bed.
  Each girl is buff, each geezer toned and strong
    charged with pulsing juice which, even yet,
fills every pair of Calvin's and each thong,
  never to be deflated, given head
    in crude games of chlamydia roulette.

Now see who comes to line the sparse grass verge,
   to toast them in Buckfast and Diamond White:
rat-boys and corn-rowed cheerleaders who urge
   them on to pull more burn-outs or to write
their donut Os, as signature, upon
   the bleached tarmac of dead suburban streets.
   There dogs set up a row and curtains twitch
as pensioners and parents telephone
   the cops to plead for quiet, sue for peace –
   tranquillity, though, is for the rich.

And so, millennia hence, you garish crock,
   when all context is lost, galleries razed
to level dust and we're long in the box,
   will future poets look on you amazed,
speculate how children might have lived when
   you were fired, lives so free and bountiful
   and there, beneath a sun a little colder,
declare *How happy were those creatures then,*
   who knew that truth was all negotiable
   and beauty in the gift of the beholder.

Anna Wigley

DÜRER'S HARE

Still trembling, after five hundred years.
Still with the smell of grass
and the blot of summer rain
on her long, thorn-tipped paws.

Look how thick the fur is,
and how each thistledown hair
catches the light
that glistens even in shadow
from the trimmed plush of the ears.

How did he keep her still?
She was crouched there long enough
for him to trace the fragile hips
and ribs beneath the mink,

to feel the pale edges
of the belly-pouch,
the sprung triggers of the flanks.
The nose shimmers
where the short hairs grow in a rosette.
Go on, touch it.

For she's only here for a moment,
Dürer's hare;
the frame can barely hold her.
Her shadow is a shifting thing,
slippery as a raincloud in wind,
and even as you look,
twitches to be gone.

Sam Willetts

TRICK

The unexceptional mystery takes place:
around eleven, love turns to matter, Dad

dead. The ward grows and shrinks, early Spring
breaking promises through the glass.

Dad's untoothed mouth gawps, and its last
O holds one darkness; dark of a worked-out

abandoned mine. His absence is brute
absurdity, his hand soft as vellum.

His new state exposes the stark child of him,
and un-sons me. No answers now to a son's

questions, about this, about the sense,
for all his slightness, of a long life's mass

coming to rest, a settling that churns up
grief in a rounding cloud. Dad

dead; end of the opaque trick
that turns our gold to lead.

CK Williams

EITHER / OR

1.

My dream after the dream of more war: that for every brain
there exists a devil, a particular devil, hairy, scaly or slimy,
but compact enough to slot between lobes, and evil, implacably evil,
slicing at us from within, causing us to yield to the part
of the soul that argues itself to pieces, then reconstitutes as a club.

When I looked closely, though, at my world, it seemed to me devils
were insufficient to account for such terror, confusion, and hatred:
evil must be other than one by one, one at a time, it has to be general,
a palpable something like carbon dioxide or ash that bleeds
over the hemispheres of the world as over the halves of the mind.

But could it really be that overarching? What of love, generosity,
pity? So I concluded there after all would have to be devils,
but mine, when I dug through the furrows to find him, seemed
    listless,
mostly he spent his time honing his horns – little pronged things
like babies' erections, but sharp, sharp as the blade that guts the goat.

2.

Just as in the brain are devils, in the world are bees: bees are angels,
angels bees. Each person has his or her bee, and his or her angel,
not "guardian angel," not either one of those with "...drawn
    swords..."
who "...inflict chastisement..." but angels of presence, the presence
that flares in the conscience not as philosophers' fire, but bees'.

Bee-fire is love, angel-fire is too: both angels and bees evolve
from seen to unseen; both as you know from your childhood
have glittering wings but regarded too closely are dragons. Both,
like trappers, have fur on their legs, sticky with lickings of pollen:
for angels the sweetness is maddening; for bees it's part of the job.

Still, not in their wildest imaginings did the angel-bees reckon
to labor like mules, be trucked from meadow to mountain,
have their compasses fouled so they'd fall on their backs,
like old men, like me, dust to their diamond, dross to their ore,
but wondering as they do who in this cruel strew of matter will
    save us.

Hugo Williams

> *'You're the top, you're an ocean liner.*
> *You're the top, you're Margaret Vyner.'*
>   Cole Porter

1. THE CULL

You sit with your address book
open on your knee,
gently but firmly
crossing out the names
of old friends who have died.
'I wonder what happened
to Kay Morrow?' you ask.
'It doesn't matter,
I never liked her really.'
Your pen hovers briefly
over the head of the bridesmaid
we've heard so much about,
then slices her in two.

You have the look of a job well done
as stragglers are rounded up
for demolition.
'Dear old Denny Moon!
He taught me to ride.
He used to jump out from behind a tree
cracking a banksia whip.
That, or driving an old Lancia
between kerosene tins.'
You shake your head at him.
In spite of all the fun
you smile with quiet satisfaction
as you let him slip away.

2. New South Wales, 1920

A hundred miles ahead of the drought
and behind on the payments
you were on your way
to start a new life in New South Wales
when the car broke down
under a coolabar tree
and your father said it was The End.

He made you get down
and wait in the shade of the tree
while he went and stood on his own.
You thought you had arrived in New South Wales
and could start to explore,
till you looked behind the tree
and saw the bush stretching away.

He brought your luggage over
to where you were sitting
and started sprinkling petrol over the car.
You thought he was cooling it down
and giving it a clean,
before you set out once more
for your new life in New South Wales.

3. Only Child

Your front wheel runs ahead of you
through the yew tree tunnels.
The berries lie in your path,
like days for you to thread.
You jam your brakes
and fly ahead of your plans.
Your elbows are grazed.
Your handlebars are askew.
Someone has to straighten them for you.

4. Someone's Girlfriend

I'd met him before, of course, at somewhere like
Government House in Sydney, then again
in a nightclub in Le Touquet, doing my nut
trying to get him to light my cigarette.
I'd heard he was going to be in this
Freddie Lonsdale play on Broadway, *Half a Loaf*,
so I got my agent to fix me an interview
with the director, Gilbert Miller,
who threw me the part of someone's girlfriend.
When your father saw me sitting there
in the dining room of the *SS Washington*,
drinking my glass of milk, he thought he'd just
discovered me. He sent a note to my table
saying 'Champagne better than milk,
why don't you join me?'
                              I remember it was evening
when we arrived in New York harbour.
Guy Middleton and Frank Lawton came down
to meet the boat in their dinner jackets
and took us back to a party. Your father and I
were staying at the Gotham, but it wasn't long
before we moved to the Devil, which was just as well,
I suppose, considering he was still married.

5. Café de Paris, 1940

I borrowed this totally embroidered
low-cut figure-hugging dress
for some charity do at the Café de Paris.
I was there to be decorative
and pose with a white pekinese,
while Lucienne Boyer sang 'Parlez-moi d'amour'.
Esmé Harmsworth won the tiara,
or someone gave it to her.

Oh, and I'll tell you who else was there,
Douglas Byng, 'The Cock of the North'.
He came on in this terrible kilt
with his usual monocle and twitch
and sang 'Flora Macdonald'.
Then there were The Yacht Club Boys:
'The huntsman said he'd found the scent.
We wondered what the huntsman meant.'

We all had to go up on stage afterwards
and Tony Kimmins, he was the organiser,
trod on my train, which immediately came off,
revealing the backs of my legs.
I let fly with a stream of invective,
which everyone heard apparently.
Tony always said he hadn't realised I was
Australian until that moment.

6. A Conjuring Trick

The undertaker slips me a folded envelope
in which he has caused to appear
her teeth and wedding ring.
His hand closes over mine.
His smile seems to require my approval
for his conjuring trick.

I feel inclined to applaud his skill
in so reducing flesh and bone
to this brief summary,
until I see his scuffed grey moccasins
and moth-eaten opera hat
with the folding mechanism showing through.

He takes me aside
and whispers that her ashes

will be waiting for me in Reception.
As we crunch back to the cars, we turn
and see smoke spiralling into the air,
while something difficult is imagined.

7. I.M. M.V.

You finally took the bait
You had cast some time before
You took the line in your mouth
You ran a mile or more

You hurled yourself in the air
You dived to the ocean floor
You came to the end of your breath
You wound yourself in to shore

Jackie Wills

Don't Commit Adultery

In a hotel room, rented flat, a friend's place, beach,
car, caravan, your own bed, his or her bed,
the children's beds, with dogs, that guy from the Red
House, your boss, on a motorbike, in a coach,

wearing that old leather jacket, after a cricket
match, in a tent, while your second child is being born,
watching a famous boxer do press ups in the gym,
while your first child is being born, after 10 shots

of Greek brandy, with someone who writes fan mail,
with your therapist, the priest, manager or director,
wife of your best friend, while your wife is having a
hysterectomy, because she has thrush, piles,

with your son's teacher, when your husband's in a coma,
with your son's girlfriend, in the Pussycat Club, with a lap
dancer, while smoking a cigar or reading the latest crap
crime fiction, contemplating Escher's prints in the Alhambra,

while your partner's leaving a message on your mobile,
by email, live webcam, wearing stiletto heels, while your wife
is undergoing radiotherapy, while flying a plane, in Fife
station, with a doctor, over the baby listening device.

Publisher acknowledgements

Patience Agbabi · EAT ME · *Bloodshot Monochrome* · Canongate

Ann Alexander · DEAD CAT POEM · *Facing Demons* · Peterloo Poets

Simon Armitage · CHAINSAW VERSUS THE PAMPAS GRASS · *The Universal Home Doctor* · Faber & Faber

Tiffany Atkinson · ZUPPA DI CECI · *Kink and Particle* · Seren

Ros Barber · MATERIAL · *Material* · 2008 · Anvil Press Poetry

Edward Barker · CRYSTAL NIGHT · *First Poems* · Baring & Rogerson

Judi Benson · BURYING THE ANCESTORS · *The Thin Places* · Rockingham Press

Kate Bingham · MONOGAMY · *Quicksand Beach* · Seren

Eavan Boland · INHERITANCE · *Domestic Violence* · Carcanet Press · Copyright © 2007 Eavan Boland

Sue Boyle · A LEISURE CENTRE IS ALSO A TEMPLE OF LEARNING · *Too Late for the Love Hotel* · Smith/Doorstop Books

Colette Bryce · EARLY VERSION · *The Full Indian Rope Trick* · Picador Poetry, an imprint of Pan Macmillan, London · Copyright © Colette Bryce 2004

John Burnside · HISTORY · *The Light Trap* · Jonathan Cape · Reprinted by permission of The Random House Group Ltd.

Matthew Caley · LINES WRITTEN UPON A PROPHYLACTIC FOUND IN A BRIXTON GUTTER · *The Scene of My Former Triumph* · Wrecking Ball Press

Ciaran Carson · THE WAR CORRESPONDENT · *Collected Poems* · 2008 · By kind permission of Ciaran Carson and The Gallery Press, Loughcrew, Oldcastle, County Meath, Ireland

Kate Clanchy · ONE, Two · *Newborn* · Picador Poetry, an imprint of Pan Macmillan, London · Copyright © Kate Clanchy 2005

Chris Considine · THE CRUELLEST CLASS · *Swaledale Sketchbook* · Smith/Doorstop Books

Wendy Cope · BEING BORING · *If I Don't Know* · Faber & Faber

Julia Copus · AN EASY PASSAGE · Magma

Allan Crosbie · MANIFESTO · *Outswimming the Eruption* · The Rialto

John F Deane · STRANGERS · *A Little Book of Hours* · 2008 · Carcanet Press

Tishani Doshi · THE DELIVERER · *Countries of the Body* · Aark Arts

Nick Drake · C/O THE SEA AT PATEA · *From the Word Go* · 2007 · Bloodaxe Books

Carol Ann Duffy · THE MAP-WOMAN · *Feminine Gospels* · Picador Poetry, an imprint of Pan Macmillan, London · Copyright © Carol Ann Duffy 2005

Ian Duhig · THE LAMMAS HIRELING · *The Lammas Hireling* · Picador Poetry, an imprint of Pan Macmillan, London · Copyright © Ian Duhig 2003

Helen Dunmore · TO MY NINE-YEAR-OLD SELF · *Glad of These Times* · 2007 · Bloodaxe Books

Douglas Dunn · THE YEAR'S AFTERNOON · *The Year's Afternoon* · Faber & Faber

Paul Durcan · THE FAR SIDE OF THE ISLAND · *The Art of Life* · Harvill Press · Reprinted by permission of The Random House Group Ltd.

UA Fanthorpe · A MINOR ROLE · *Queueing for the Sun* · Peterloo Poets

Helen Farish · PROGRAMME · *Intimates* · Jonathan Cape · Reprinted by permission of The Random House Group Ltd.

Paul Farley · LIVERPOOL DISAPPEARS FOR A BILLIONTH OF A SECOND · *Tramp in Flames* · Picador Poetry, an imprint of Pan Macmillan, London · Copyright © Paul Farley 2006

Vicki Feaver · THE GUN · *The Book of Blood* · Jonathan Cape · Reprinted by permission of The Random House Group Ltd.

Leontia Flynn · THE FURTHEST DISTANCES I'VE TRAVELLED · *These Days* · Jonathan Cape · Reprinted by permission of The Random House Group Ltd.

Roderick Ford · GIUSEPPE · *The Shoreline of Falling* · Bradshaw Books

Linda France · COOKING WITH BLOOD · *The Simultaneous Dress* · Bloodaxe Books

Tom French · NIGHT DRIVE · *Touching the Bones* · 2001 · By kind permission of Tom French and The Gallery Press, Loughcrew, Oldcastle, County Meath, Ireland

John Fuller · MY LIFE ON THE MARGINS OF CELEBRITY · *Song & Dance* · Chatto & Windus · Reprinted by permission of The Random House Group Ltd.

Lydia Fulleylove · NIGHT DRIVE · *Notes on Sea and Land* · 2011 · Happen*Stance*

John Goodby · THE UNCLES · *A True Prize* · Cinnamon Press

Vona Groarke · BODKIN · *Spindrift* · 2009 · By kind permission of Vona Groarke and The Gallery Press, Loughcrew, Oldcastle, County Meath, Ireland

Paul Groves · MAN AND BOY · Poetry Wales

Jen Hadfield · SONG OF PARTS · *Almanacs* · 2005 · Bloodaxe Books

Michael Hamburger · THE DOG-DAYS INTERRUPTED · *Wild and Wounded* · 2004 · Anvil Press Poetry

Sophie Hannah · GOD'S ELEVENTH HOUR · *First of the Last Chances* · 2003 · Carcanet Press

David Harsent · STREET SCENES · *Legion* · Faber & Faber

Seamus Heaney · OUT OF THE BAG · *Electric Light* · Faber & Faber

David Herd · SEPTEMBER 11TH, 2001 · *Mandelson! Mandelson! A Memoir* · 2005 · Carcanet Press

Ellen Hinsey · XVII CORRESPONDENCES: APHORISMS REGARDING IMPATIENCE · *Update on the Descent* · 2009 · Bloodaxe Books

Mick Imlah · THE AYRSHIRE ORPHEUS · *The Lost Leader* · Faber& Faber

AB Jackson · FILING · *Fire Stations* · 2003 · Anvil Press Poetry

Kathleen Jamie · SPEIRIN · *The Tree House* · Picador Poetry, an imprint of Pan Macmillan, London · Copyright © Kathleen Jamie 2004

Alan Jenkins · EFFECTS · *A Shorter Life* · Chatto & Windus · Reprinted by permission of The Random House Group Ltd.

Emma Jones · SONNET · *The Striped World* · Faber & Faber

Jackie Kay · LATE LOVE · *Darling: New & Selected Poems* · 2007 · Bloodaxe Books

Judy Kendall · WA, HARMONY · *Joy Change* · Cinnamon Press

John Kinsella · THE HIERARCHY OF SHEEP – A REPORT FROM MY BROTHER · Fremantle

Nick Laird · THE LAYERED · *To a Fault* · Faber & Faber

Michael Laskey · THE PAIN ON HIS FACE · *Permission to Breathe* · Smith/ Doorstop Books

Gwyneth Lewis · MOTHER TONGUE · *Chaotic Angels: Poems in English* · 2005 · Bloodaxe Books

Michael Longley · THE HOLLY BUSH · *A Hundred Doors* · Jonathan Cape · Reprinted by permission of The Random House Group Ltd.

Mary MacRae · JURY · *As Birds Do* · Second Light

Derek Mahon · ROMANCE · *An Autumn Wind* · 2010 · By kind permission of Derek Mahon and The Gallery Press, Loughcrew, Oldcastle, County Meath, Ireland

Lorraine Mariner · THURSDAY · *Furniture* · Picador Poetry, an imprint of Pan Macmillan, London · Copyright © Lorraine Mariner 2009

Ruth Padel · You, Shiva and My Mum · *Voodoo Shop* · Chatto & Windus ·
Reprinted by permission of The Random House Group Ltd.
Don Paterson · Song for Natalie 'Tusja' Beridze · *Rain* · Faber & Faber
Clare Pollard · Thinking of England · *Bedtime* · 2002 · Bloodaxe Books
Jacob Polley · The Cheapjack · *Little Gods* · Picador Poetry, an imprint of
Pan Macmillan, London · Copyright © Jacob Polley 2006
Andrea Porter · Assassinations · *A Season of Small Insanities* · Salt
Peter Porter · Last Words · *Max is Missing* · Picador, an imprint of
Pan Macmillan, London
Richard Price · *from* A Spelthorne Bird List · *Lucky Day* · 2005 ·
Carcanet Press
Sheenagh Pugh · Night Nurses in the Morning · *The Beautiful Lie* · Seren
Sally Read · Instruction · *The Point of Splitting* · 2005 · Bloodaxe Books
Robin Robertson · La Stanza Delle Mosche · *Swithering* · Picador
Poetry, an imprint of Pan Macmillan, London · Copyright © Robin
Robertson 2006
Fiona Sampson · From the Adulteress's Songbook · *Rough Music* ·
2010 · Carcanet Press
Myra Schneider · Goulash · *Circling the Core* · Enitharmon Press
Jo Shapcott · Of Mutability · *Of Mutability* · Faber & Faber
Kathryn Simmonds · The Boys in the Fish Shop · *Sunday at the Skin
Launderette* · Seren
Catherine Smith · The New Bride · *The New Bride* · Smith/Doorstop
Books
John Stammers · Ask Them · *Stolen Love Behaviour* · Picador, an imprint
of Pan Macmillan, London · Copyright © John Stammers 2005
George Szirtes · Song · *New & Collected Poems* · 2008 · Bloodaxe Books
Adam Thorpe · On Her Blindness · *Birds with a Broken Wing* · Jonathan
Cape · Reprinted by permission of The Random House Group Ltd.
Tim Turnbull · Ode on a Grayson Perry Urn · *Caligula on Ice and Other
Poems* · 2009 · Donut Press
Anna Wigley · Dürer's Hare · *Dürer's Hare* · 2005 · Gomer Press
Sam Willetts · Trick · *New Light for the Old Dark* · Jonathan Cape ·
Reprinted by permission of The Random House Group Ltd.
CK Williams · Either / Or · *Wait* · 2011 · Bloodaxe Books
Hugo Williams · Poems to My Mother · *West End Final* · Faber & Faber
Jackie Wills · Don't Commit Adultery · *Commandments* · Arc Publications

Winners of the Forward Prizes 2001-2010

BEST COLLECTION

2010 · Seamus Heaney · *Human Chain* · Faber & Faber

2009 · Don Paterson · *Rain* · Faber & Faber

2008 · Mick Imlah · *The Lost Leader* · Faber & Faber

2007 · Sean O'Brien · *The Drowned Book* · Picador Poetry

2006 · Robin Robertson · *Swithering* · Picador Poetry

2005 · David Harsent · *Legion* · Faber & Faber

2004 · Kathleen Jamie · *The Tree House* · Picador Poetry

2003 · Ciaran Carson · *Breaking News* · The Gallery Press

2002 · Peter Porter · *Max is Missing* · Picador Poetry

2001 · Sean O'Brien · *Downriver* · Picador Poetry

BEST FIRST COLLECTION

2010 · Hilary Menos · *Berg* · Seren

2009 · Emma Jones · *The Striped World* · Faber & Faber

2008 · Kathryn Simmons · *Sunday at the Skin Launderette* · Seren

2007 · Daljit Nagra · *Look We Have Coming to Dover!* · Faber & Faber

2006 · Tishani Doshi · *Countries of the Body* · Aark Arts

2005 · Helen Farish · *Intimates* · Cape Poetry

2004 · Leontia Flynn · *These Days* · Cape Poetry

2003 · AB Jackson · *Fire Stations* · Anvil Press

2002 · Tom French · *Touching the Bones* · The Gallery Press

2001 · John Stammers · *Panoramic Lounge-Bar* · Picador Poetry

BEST SINGLE POEM

2010 · Julia Copus · AN EASY PASSAGE · *Magma*

2009 · Robin Robertson · AT ROANE HEAD · *London Review of Books*

2008 · Don Paterson · LOVE POEM FOR NATALIE "TUSJA" BERIDZE ·
The Poetry Review

2007 · Alice Oswald · DUNT · *Poetry London*

2006 · Sean O'Brien · FANTASIA ON A THEME OF JAMES WRIGHT ·
The Poetry Review

2005 · Paul Farley · LIVERPOOL DISAPPEARS FOR A BILLIONTH OF A SECOND
· *The North*

2004 · Daljit Nagra · Look We Have Coming to Dover! · *The Poetry Review*

2003 · Robert Minhinnick · The Fox in the Museum of Wales · *Poetry London*

2002 · Medbh McGuckian · She Is in the Past, She Has This Grace · *The Shop*

2001 · Ian Duhig · The Lammas Hireling · National Poetry Competition

For more detail and further reading about Forward Prizes' alumni, see www.forwardartsfoundation.org, Facebook.com/forwardprizes or @forwardprizes